TOXIC HUSBANDS

BREAK FREE OF YOUR DYSFUNCTIONAL
MARRIAGE AND BEGIN LIVING A MENTALLY
HEALTHY LIFESTYLE.

CHELSEA LOXLEY

This book is dedicated to my cousin Tiffany G.

*A healthy relationship will **never** require you to sacrifice your friends, your dream, or your dignity.*

— Our Mindful Life

CONTENTS

Bonus free gift just for you!   vi

Preface   xii

Introduction   xiii

Chapter 1   1
WHY WOMEN FALL FOR TOXIC MEN

Chapter 2   23
TOXIC BEHAVIOR AWARENESS

Chapter 3   35
MASCULINITY VS. TOXIC MASCULINITY

Chapter 4   47
TOXIC REINDEER GAMES

Chapter 5   65
SEX WITH A SOMATIC NARCISSIST HUSBAND

Chapter 6   81
PLANNING YOUR EXIT STRATEGY

Chapter 7   91
LEVEL UP

Chapter 8   106
HELPING CHILDREN COPE WITH THE DIVORCE

Chapter 9   126
ENJOYING YOUR FREEDOM

Conclusion   135

Just for you!   137

Acknowledgements   139

About the Author   143

If you enjoyed this book: 145

**BONUS FREE GIFT JUST
FOR YOU!**

You may question yourself about why you would want
a copy of my guide: "Fix Your Crown, a Femininity

Manifesto." Allow me to explain. If a woman is feminine, she will most likely attract a masculine male. Assume you are fighting to get in touch with your femininity or are worrying about being more feminine. In that case, I urge you to download my manifesto and discover how to live correctly in your center (again, some women are masculine at their core). As a whole, most women are genuinely feminine at their center. I'm not sitting here telling you that there are a ton of rules for being feminine. For example, you do not have to do the washing and cleaning to be feminine. You can still be feminine without doing these things. Also, you are not immediately feminine just because you wear dresses all the time and wear long hair (although I believe keeping your hair long is immensely helpful for achieving a feminine 'image'). Nevertheless, you can still be very feminine with short hair or a bob (take, for example, Halle Berry, Beyonce, Anne Hathaway, and Lucy Hale when they do a short hairstyle).

Femininity is Not. About. Rules. Rules = rigid, and a feminine woman is not tough! Femininity is about being FREE. Free to be yourself authentic self, free to love who you want, and be loved by others. Free not to judge people, free to enjoy the best for others, free to be understanding, free to lead and not follow, free to believe rather than doubt, free to be a power for good, free to be catering, and most importantly, free to love yourself.

By free, I mean not being confined in your negative views and not deceiving yourself, which will prevent you from fulfilling your entire life's potential. Ultimately, you are here because you may want more, and you want to learn. I think all of us want more. The only obstacle to having more is within yourself – the perspective you have on something. You can have a mindset that empowers you – or you can have a mentality that disempowers you or doesn't serve you.

If I may give my viewpoint, I'd say we are all here to become the best we can be. Once you are free from hurt, you are much more able to have satisfying relationships with your man, being a better friend, a better mother, a better daughter, sister, girlfriend, wife, no matter what role you play. That is why my femininity manifesto is this book, to help you accomplish all of those things.

If a woman doesn't feel free, she will exude this heavy, dark kind of energy that does not care to encourage men (or women) to want to be near to them. You've probably met many women who give out this kind of energy, too.

What is The One most distinctively emotional trigger within every man in this Universe that motivates Him to desire and WANT to Commit to One Woman, take care of her, worship her, and only Her? Femininity Starts From inside our bodies.

You can wear pants and be feminine. You can wear business suits and be feminine. You can still wear jeans, camo pants, hoodies, tracksuits, whatever – and be still feminine. As I mentioned earlier, being feminine is about who you are from inside your body. If you radiate the energy of feminine freedom, softness, and happiness, you can literally wear a brown paper bag, and you'll still be feminine.

It has very little to do with your appearance. Whatever your style is, there are men and women out there who will find you attractive, gorgeous, and beautiful. I do suggest dressing traditionally feminine. Anyway, my point is that this does not necessarily prevent you from being a feminine woman, for example? Do you think that men can still be masculine with long hair? Of course, they can!

Although wearing dresses, perfume, ribbons, bows, long hair, earrings, heels, etc. – are an immediate visual cue for femininity. You are, however, not limited to one way of doing things to become more feminine. Suppose you can stimulate your man intellectually, mentally, spiritually, sexually, inspire him to grow, become better, do more, and achieve much more success and happiness – trust me. In that case, you are worth a whole lot more than the perfect physical 'canvas' of a woman that has no substance inside. And, more often than not, it's the empty vessel that makes a ton of noise.

Now do not get this twisted – just because I say femininity is about freedom, I do not mean that a woman consistently wants freedom. I mean that a genuinely feminine woman is not stuck in her head with disempowering beliefs. In any case, a critical part of feminine energy wants to be possessed by her man. Don't all of us women desire to be accepted? We all want a strong, masculine man who knows what he wants and is confident enough to go and get it. Not just that, but he is secure, intelligent, and stable enough to LEAD his Woman. If a man is always soft and gentle to you (without any other substance), that gets stale and boring after a while, right?! It's like watching paint dry. I have mentioned previously that you should dress in feminine clothing that suits you, and if you want to keep your ideal man for life, your physical image is essential. It helps us immensely to appear feminine on the outside, but you do not have to. It is all about having grace, and most importantly, exuding self-confidence.

You can still participate in sports and be feminine. It is HOW you do it that determines whether you're more manly or more womanly. Sure, there are sports that I would recommend staying away from for a feminine woman because it's sometimes tough to play those particular sports in a feminine manner, but most of them are ok.

You are not a one-dimensional person. You can go for a long run or play golf, but do it in a feminine way (a woman who thrives in her feminine sexual essence will do this naturally).

Also – there are masculine traits to every Woman. We need masculine energy too, and it keeps us balanced; we can get things done and move forward. When I was Retail Operations Manager, you can bet I was in a more masculine mode! Masculine energy is very FOCUSED, and feminine energy tends to fluctuate more.

Women can also do loads of things at once, but men generally work a whole lot better when focusing on one thing. And believe me, I would have *loved* to be able to focus on just my sales, but I had to multitask. I got through, but my work hours did terrible things to balance my relationship with my man. He hated me working so much. Honestly, those were the times when our passion dwindled in the relationship.

So, every Woman would ideally have a very well-developed masculine facet to her personality, and every man would ideally have a very well-developed feminine side to his character. Although, of course, most feminine women's character will be absorbed by feminine energy.

If you are genuinely interested in discovering more about what feminine traits are, I've done an overnight guide – please click on the image.

Thank YOU, and stay fabulous!

PREFACE

~

I have decided to write my life story because I wanted to share what I have learned in life with the World. I also wanted to give a little bit of the history of my marriage, who I once was, and who I have become.

It is my story; it is not perfect in any way, but that's cool.

I hope that my story helps women feel good about themselves, learn to live life in beautiful ways and discover something about toxic people around us. We will grow through this process together, and there is life after a divorce.

~Chelsea Loxley
   contact@chelsealoxley.com

INTRODUCTION

~

"I want a divorce, and you had better sign those papers by the time I get back!"

Hollered Jason as he banged the kitchen door behind him. Irene stood by the window and watched his car disappear down the hill. He was on his way out for the evening to hang with the fellas, and she was sure he would not return home until he was drunk. She looked down at the divorce papers Jason had stuffed into her hands.

Earlier that evening, Jason had arrived home from work and seemed irritated; after coming inside, he dropped his briefcase on the floor by the kitchen door, which is an alternate entrance to their 4,000 square foot home. He showered, changed his clothes, and left after giving her the papers. Irene felt her knees turning to jelly as she collapsed on the floor and let out her pain in a bloodcurdling scream.

She could not help but remember the good memories of when they were still young and in love. Jason was a charming 24-year-old, and Irene was 22 at that time. They met in college, graduated, and right away, Jason began his career as a college professor at one of the nearby colleges. They had married a year later, and Irene became a stay-at-home mother. After five years passed, she could not recognize her husband anymore.

He had turned into a narcissistic monster. Irene's friends had warned her that Jason was too good to be true, but his charm had blinded her. He ruined her life, and she didn't know what to do or how to start again. It all began when they stopped talking. He began to shut down her opinions and ignore her requests.

She did not realize when she became an object to him. Then the cheating started. He made her believe that he began to cheat because she was the problem. So, she started working out more to get rid of the weight from having children. She updated her wardrobe and also began to wear sexy lingerie. She took care of her body and made sure to look sexy for him. She got a book on the Kama Sutra and learned all she could about tantric sex.

At first, her husband seemed to return his affections for her, and which revived their sex life. But after a few months, the nightmare began. He started keeping late nights and taking trips. At first, he respected her enough to keep it a secret from her. But soon, he began to flaunt his cheating in her face.

She remembered his first beating. He had apologized to her and tried to make amends, but it never changed anything. She had thought of leaving many times, but she lacked the courage.

How would she pick up the pieces of her life again? Where would she go? Could she face her family and friends?

Now, she had no choice. Jason did not care about her or their three children, and she knew that he would make her life a living nightmare if she did not sign the divorce papers.

Irene stood up from the living room floor and went to her bedroom. She could not feel or do anything. She just sat down on the bed and stared into space.

Does Irene's situation sound familiar to you? You married a man you thought you knew, and many years down the line, you find yourself in a very toxic relationship with a narcissistic person. You did not know how or when everything went downhill. You're recently divorced, and you have no idea of how to move on. You do not know how to take care of your kids or how to move on with your life.

Some of you are carrying your families' burden, and you are about to crumble under pressure. I know exactly how you feel. I know this because I went through the same thing. I was once an Irene. I have been an Irene. When I got divorced after over twenty years of marriage, I thought my life was over. I had two children, and I did not know how to put my life together.

After seven years of studying and taking several courses on human behavior, relationships and counseling, I have gotten my life back. I also help thousands of women who have been in toxic relationships and struggling with getting over a divorce to learn how to love themselves and achieve their dreams.

In this book, you'll learn not only how to get your groove back and fall in love with yourself, but you'll also learn how to navigate through the aftermath of a divorce. If you are struggling with how to leave a toxic relationship, I will help you find your courage and strength to take your life back. You will also learn how to spot a toxic Husband's signs and avoid getting into a relationship that will make you miserable.

One of the reasons why we often fall into toxic Relationships is because we cannot recognize the signs of what they are. I will show you what the indicators are, and how to spot these signs, and how they manipulate women. I will also explain how you can deal with toxic men with grace, dignity, and femininity. You will learn how to manage the toxic men in your life without losing your sense of self or lowering your self-worth.

I can say this boldly because I have studied extensively on toxic behavior. I understand how much it hurts to lose yourself and not know how to move on. I know how it can be effortless to fall into the trap of blame yourself for your partner's behavior, but I've good news for you: you are not to blame. It is not because of you that he is physically abusive or that he cheated on you. You are not to blame for the divorce!

You are a wonderful, amazing woman who has so much to offer. You can heal from this because I did, and I will share what helped me heal.

Right now, I am happy and doing the things I love. There was a time when my life fell apart, and I couldn't look forward to another day. It took a journey of healing and self-love to get to where I am today. This book is your first step to a remarkable journey of self-love, self-discovery, and healing.

By the time you are done reading this book, you will not only realize how wonderful you are, but I will also provide you with enough knowledge to identify toxic behaviors and also help other women in unhealthy relationships. So, take my hand, flip the page and let's get your groove back!

∾

CHAPTER 1

WHY WOMEN FALL FOR TOXIC MEN

*M*any women enter into a toxic relationship because they have no idea what it is. Some women still enter into one knowing that their men are toxic. Despite knowing how dangerous, unhealthy relationships are, many young women attract them. So why do we keep falling for the wrong men? Unfortunately, there is no simple answer to this question. First of all, we have to analyze how the media portrays toxic relationships.

*T*oxic relationships and the media.
You will find unhealthy relationships throughout the media, especially in movies and tv shows. There are the more common examples like Kelly and Ryan from the office or Harley Quinn and the Joker from The Suicide Squad, but there are other less apparent instances of couples we look up to.

As we grow in life, we discover that couples such as Chuck and Blair from "Gossip Girl" or Edward and Bella from "Twilight" are pretty toxic, but we all adored them as teens. As teenagers, our brains were still developing and watching such relationships without understanding how unhealthy they have damaged our perceptions of romantic relationships. Some of the most popular and beloved relationships popular like Ross and Rachel from "Friends", have toxic tendencies. In time, we begin to think these behaviors are normal because of how often we see them. It makes it more difficult for us to recognize toxic relationships.

*H*ow toxic relationships affect our health. It should not be surprising that toxic relationships can cause mental health problems like depression and anxiety, but they can lead to physical health risks. According to Sherrie Bourg Carter, "In a long-term study that followed more than 10,000 subjects for an average of 12.2 years, researchers determined that people in negative relationships were at a greater risk for developing heart problems. Including a fatal cardiac event than counterparts whose close relationships were not negative." This information is scary, but it shows that healthy relationships are just as crucial for your physical health as your mental health.

. . .

*W*hy are young women attracted to toxic men?

Since toxic relationships are so dangerous to our mental and physical health, why are young women attracted to toxic men? There are several explanations, but the two significant reasons women fall for toxic men are that they believe they can fix them and become addicted to such relationships.

Women who love to see the best in people habitually fall into the "I can fix him" trap. They get drawn into toxic relationships. According to columnist and breakup coach Chelsea Leigh Truscott, "for someone who suffers from rescuer syndrome or savior complex, nothing engages their heart more than a person who is toxic and could use some help."

Have you ever been in a friendship with someone who insists on being in a relationship with a guy who is not good for her, but she is determined to fix him? Or perhaps that is the reason you are in a relationship with that toxic man? While it is perfect for an entertaining romantic comedy, that is not what true love is. These movies and tv shows are not what healthy relationships are. Seeing someone and wanting to change them is not a sign of love. Healthy relationships bring out the best in each other, but they are also about loving someone for who they are, including their flaws.

. . .

*a*dditionally, toxic relationships are addictive. We will explore these reasons later in the chapter. For relationship coach Cherlyn Chong, we can become so addicted that we are willing to sacrifice our whole life for five minutes of exhilaration.

Dr. Helen Fisher, a renowned behavioral expert, calls it the "Frustration attraction phenomenon, where the unpredictability heightens those feelings of romantic love instead of hindering them."

Toxic men usually reward women for what they term as "good behavior" with the woman's affection so desperately desires, filling her brain with dopamine. She then becomes addicted to the euphoria that the dopamine gives and then crashes when he goes back to toxic behavior, only to get another "high" the next time her partner rewards her "good behavior" with his affection.

Unfortunately, this is why toxic relationships are very addictive.

Here are some other reasons why women fall for toxic men:

1. They are a temporary cure for boredom.

Sometimes, when you have a dry spell or feel bored, you feel the need to get your groove back. What is the first thing you do? You get into a relationship but not with the nice guy who buys you coffee; you reach for the dangerous, wild one who makes your heart beat faster. Your friends and family think you are crazy for being with a guy just because he is great in bed or he makes you believe that you are the only woman in the world. Even though he will eventually leave, you are happy with the way he makes you feel. You are living in the moment and enjoying every inch of excitement. Ultimately, the excitement will turn into disappointment or heartbreak. The next time you feel bored, go on a trip, go to the spa, and travel to a great place you've always wanted to visit.

2. You are afraid of a real relationship.

The friendly, stable guys are the epitome of committed relationships. Still, suppose you are not interested in a committed relationship right now. In that case, you are going to turn away from them and go for someone else like the hot guy who would preferably get a tattoo on his abs than be in an exclusive relationship. For some reason, you believe that you can leave your heart at home and have mad fun without getting hurt. You might even tell yourself, "I do not want a stable relationship with him or anyone, so this works perfectly for me!" But does it? Perhaps something inside is wishing that he will become boyfriend material.

3. You want to be the one to fix him.

Perhaps you do not like nice guys, but you are secretly attracted to the bad boy who may change because of you. So, you date a toxic guy in the hopes of changing him into a white knight. You want to be the one to make him see the light and become a committed partner. You think he will love you forever for it. Here is the thing: men like this never change, so do not waste your time.

4. You feel like you have something to prove.

Toxic men can help you prove that you are worthy and deserve to be loved. Although the guys in your past mistreated you or had an absentee father, this new guy is different and constantly validates you. The problem here is that bringing more bad boys into your life will make you vulnerable to further rejection. It would be best if you were not opening the door for them but slamming it in their faces instead. You do not need validation from anyone.

5. You think they are no good guys left.

Sometimes, it looks like Good guys are an endangered species, so falling in love with a good guy seems like an impossible dream. So, you would willingly stick with the guy who leaves you hanging, keeps getting you upset, or cheats on you. You believe that this is as good as it will get. You will never meet a good guy until you dump the bad ones.

6. You are in an attraction-frustration cycle.

When a guy gives you lots of attention and makes you feel special, your brain releases a good dose of dopamine, a feel-good hormone that surprisingly flows more when you get approval from the guy. When a toxic guy is showering you with attention and then suddenly goes AWOL, you will be looking for him to return so you can experience that dopamine hit instead of getting away a far away from him as possible. This is similar to how you would act if you were a drug addict in need of a quick fix.

7. You want him because he is forbidden.

The series Fifty Shades is partly to blame for this one. Bad boys are like that devilish chocolate cake you would rather eat instead of a tomato salad. They are delicious yet forbidden because you know that they are not good for you, but you cannot resist having a taste. In the same way, you might disregard the fact that you need to cut down calories; you will ignore your gut telling you to leave that toxic guy.

8. You cannot resist the hot, crazy sex.

Research published in the sex and marital therapy journal discovered that women often associate that bad boy giving you the eye at the club with great sex. When scientists asked college-aged women what they felt about nice guys, both discovered that even though women like dating nice guys, when they want great sex, they all turn to the bad boys. In chapter four, I will discuss why sex with toxic men seems so addictive.

Breaking the cycle

Patterns of toxic relationships are not easy to break because the victim's brain has become desensitized by unhealthy behavior. Shahida Arabi, the author of Power: Surviving and Thriving after Narcissistic Abuse, believes "Our minds can become masochists, seeking the very people that hurt them. They grow so accustomed to good behavior from nice guys that they stop releasing as much dopamine. That is why also in a healthy relationship, we can become so "used to" the safety and security of a gentle partner that we find him or her less exciting over time."

The surest way to break the pattern of toxic relationships is by developing a healthy relationship with yourself. It would be best if you discovered your dignity and worth. Get to know yourself and learn how to set boundaries. Take time to find yourself, even if it is something as simple as meditating every night or doing a weekly facial. If you love yourself and exude confidence, you will attract good men to show you what true love is.

It is also necessary to know the signs of a toxic relationship so that you can guard your heart. I will discuss more on unhealthy behavior in the next chapter. Still, the most common traits of a toxic relationship are abuse of power and control, demandingness, selfishness, insecurity, self-centeredness, criticism, negativity, dishonesty, distrust, demeaning comments and attitudes, and jealousy. Many toxic relationships start well, so it gets more challenging to leave when things get rough.

*I*t is not surprising that toxic relationships have become standard in our culture, making it a difficult habit for many young women to break. Learning how to love yourself and developing good relationship habits will take time, but it is worth it in the end if you want to have a healthy relationship. First of all, you have to learn how low self-esteem can affect your relationships.

The effect of low self-esteem affects women in relationships.

Nothing inhibits your ability to have an authentic, mutual relationship like low self-esteem. If you do not believe you are good enough, how do you expect a loving man to choose you? Low self-esteem will make you sabotage relationships that have potential or settle for men that treat you the way you treat yourself. But low self-esteem does not always display itself in the same way in every relationship.

Here are the ten most common ways that low self-esteem can manifest in your relationship.

1. Bring the bling.

You feel inadequate and constantly dream about a knight in shining armor that will take you out of your circumstances and make everything in your life better. This longing may have formed because you lacked a father figure in your life. You may think that you know why your father was never there to "save" you. You believe that your father was never there because of you. Or perhaps you did have a father who lavished attention on you, and now you want to feel that way in all your relationships. So, you may feel obliged to cling to the fantasy of perfection as the standard you established for your romantic partners to live up to. Unfortunately, they cannot. Even if your partner is solid, consistent, and loving, you may dismiss his efforts and find ways to sabotage the relationship.

2. Testing

Why would he love me? Maybe he does not love me, does he? Under the surface, these insecurities take over your emotions and actions. You cannot believe someone can truly love you, so you test your partner every chance you get so that he can prove his love for you (which you do not even believe or trust anyway). You may even end the relationship because you know your partner will inevitably leave. The end of every relationship allows you to say, "See, I knew it all along. I am unlovable." unfortunately, there is intense regret in the aftermath when you lose a good man this way.

3. Guarded

If your parents had a painful divorce or were unfaithful to each other, you might feel unable to trust a partner now, whether you are conscious of your suspicion or not. You may be uncertain and afraid of allowing yourself to love so that you leave your partner before they can abandon you, or you will not let yourself get fully committed in a relationship in the first place. Without believing that perhaps he won't betray you, you are terrified of exposing yourself to the possibility of being hurt.

4. Resilient

Despite situations that could contribute to low self-esteem, some women are just naturally resilient. They are either born that way or work hard to acquire that trait – despite negative experiences – to engage in a positive, substantive relationship as they mature. Perhaps someone in her life gave her guidance and support and helped her offset her low self-esteem with resilience. Resilience allows women to be more meticulous in their approach to men rather than hysterical about it.

5. Man-crazy

When you have low self-esteem, it can seem as though nothing comes easily or naturally to you. Instead, because you do not believe that you are inherently lovable, you feel like you have to fight and claw and strive for love. You feel like if you do not go a million extra miles for something, you are never going to get it. Unfortunately, this can lead you to become obsessed, consumed, and fascinated with your love interest in a way that ruins the ability to have a healthy relationship. You are already so far ahead. When the relationship doesn't develop as quickly or as fast as you can, it is not easy to tolerate. Instead, this is your cue to work even more complicated. Just realize that it is difficult for the man to sustain that level of intensity right from the start with you, and it may be a more intense experience than he prepares for.

Are you ready to surrender your hopes for a real connection with a partner to guarantee wealth and financial safety? This type manifests as the need to hook a mate with looks or sex, or other physical resources while hiding what you believe is a shameful inner part of yourself. It also gives you the emotional safety of control: you are in charge of your ability to please a man without having to provide him with your heart. It is not the same with the rescue fantasy in that you don't expect to be swept off your feet by an illusion but to have the assurance of financial security at the cost of other feelings you may have.

7. Seeking insecurity

Since you are familiar with situations that create low self-esteem – being abandoned, being cheated on, etc. – you will settle for relationships in which you can feel this everyday insecurity. When it is not there, you will want to create it. If the relationship gets too secure, you may lose interest and get bored. You may eventually leave the relationship. You are so used to working to keep an insecure connection that these types of relationships become the only ones you seek. But, simultaneously, a deeper part of you tries to push your relationship to the brink of collapse and go back again so you can create that atmosphere of insecurity.

8. Settlers

You are ready to commit yourself to the person who shows interest in you. You get less meticulous with relationships. You may even be prepared to condone behavior that does not satisfy you because you feel lucky to have been chosen by anyone at all, even though you are aware that something is wrong or that you are not happy.

9. Afraid of Intimacy

Did you experience intimacy and connection in

your family while growing up? If not, these experiences may become uncomfortable now. You may become frightened as the relationship progresses because a real connection feels so foreign and fake. Instead of accepting this connection, you may back away and become emotionally distant, and shut down sexually.

10. Disbelief

It can be challenging to imagine and believe that you can create and sustain real connections. To protect yourself, you accept dishonesty even from an honest partner, which ruins the relationship as it goes on. Then, as you distrust your partner so often, maybe even persistently, he may start to consider lying a workable option – he is "doing time," so why not commit the crime? It, in turn, confirms your belief that you can trust no one.

*W*e all know there are many more ways women express low self-esteem in their relationships. But sometimes, the self-knowledge gotten by assessing a list like this will help you understand not only parts of who you are but also parts of who you are not. Self-knowledge can help you stay away from some of these low self-esteem patterns in relationships and move toward understanding, accepting, and integrating your emotions, beliefs, and behaviors. Acknowledging how your actions have been affected by your past can help you create a real connection with the right person and have a healthy relationship.

*B*uilding self-esteem.
The year I got divorced was a tough one for me. I was battling with my mental health and also suffering from depression and anxiety. When I looked around at other beautiful, successful women, I asked myself: how do they do it? How do people manage to feel so good about themselves? Don't they have problems?

I needed to find out, and I wanted to share my findings with other women who, like me, wanted to feel happy and at peace with themselves. So, I went all out and did tons of research and took several courses. I grew and developed my hobbies, and with time, I got my self-confidence back. I have compiled a list of some self-love tips that will help you fall in love with yourself.

*S*wap negative with positive thinking.
Recognize the triggers: to increase the level of positive thinking in your everyday life, and you first have to recognize the people, places, and activities that promote negative thinking. Maybe it is your bank balance, or perhaps it is a colleague who is constantly complaining. You cannot change some situations, but you can change how you react to them and understand

them. It begins with paying attention to what makes you feel sad or anxious.

Pay attention to your inner self-talk: there is a constant dialogue, or "self-talk," going on in your brain as you go about your daily activities. This self-talk takes in the atmosphere around you and makes assessments about yourself and others. So, observe any exciting trends in this dialogue. Is this train of thought based on facts? Or is it usually favoring towards the irrational or constantly assuming the worst in every situation?

Challenge your thinking: if you catch yourself jumping to conclusions or constantly toning down the positive things about yourself, you have to step up and add some positive review to your self-talk. Learning how to focus on the positive and encourage yourself is similar to strengthening a muscle. You have to use your brain a little every day to develop a capability for positive thinking, to forgive yourself when you make mistakes, and to learn how to give yourself credit when you succeed at anything.

*T*ake Inventory.
    If you are unsure where you are when it comes to your self-esteem, taking an inventory of your personal qualities and strengths can help. If you discover that you are listing more weaknesses than strengths, this may be a sign that you are too hard on yourself. Think about the talents, abilities, and

passions you have not listed or probably have not even discovered yet. Do not pretend you know everything about yourself or what you are capable of doing. People with high self-esteem allow room for self-discovery every day.

*a*cknowledge Your Successes.
Usually, people with low self-esteem will attribute their successes to luck or chance. Or they may focus on not being perfect rather than acknowledging how far they have come. People with high self-esteem take the time to applaud themselves and celebrate their accomplishments. They say "thank you" when people give them compliments rather than dismissing them. It does not mean that people with high self-esteem are proud, arrogant, or selfish; they believe in their abilities and acknowledge successes when they do happen.

*D*o Not Compare Yourself to Others.
We are programmed to be competitive, so comparing ourselves to others comes naturally to us. But it can be harmful. There is no reason for you to compare yourself to anyone else on the planet because there is only one you. Instead, pay attention to develop yourself and your journey. This shift of energy, alone, will give you a sense of freedom.

Do Not Worry About other People's Opinions:

In that same way, do not bother about what society believes or expects of you. You cannot make everybody happy; it is impossible and a total waste of time. It will only slow you down on your journey to being the best version of yourself.

*S*tay healthy with balance and diet.
There is a strong mind-body connection, so whenever we are feeling physically healthy, it can have a profound impact on our self-esteem, as well as our emotions.

Mindful eating and exercise are incredibly vital to your health. If you are not healthy, it will affect other aspects of your life. It will hamper your self-esteem and lead to further emotional consequences. Select exercises that will make you feel good about yourself.

Even small movements, such as yoga, can increase your serotonin levels and help you feel calmer, enable you to make better decisions, make you feel more robust, and feel more in control of your life.

*M*ake a list of your goals and priorities.
Make a habit of listing your goals each day, week, or month. Try to stick to them, so you do not get distracted by other people's needs, demands, and requests.

Pause and evaluate before automatically saying "yes" to any request.

When you receive any request, think to yourself, "Is this something you can do or something you want to do? Are you saying yes because this is something you want to do or just so that the person will like, need, or approve of me?

*a*llow yourself to make mistakes.
We have been told right from when we were young that "nobody's perfect, everyone makes mistakes." But the older we get, the more pressure we feel to avoid failure. Give yourself a break. There is zero wrong with making mistakes, so you can learn and grow from them. Accept and embrace your past. You are constantly changing and extending from the person you once were into who you are today and who you will be one day. So, disregard that voice in your head that says you must be perfect. Make mistakes — lots of them! The lessons you will gain are priceless.

*R*emember, your value is not in the way your body looks.
It is a fundamental truth! Many things in the world will try to distract you from this powerful truth. Sometimes even your own internalized sexism encourages your thoughts of inadequacy. You are deserving because of who you are and not because of your body. So, wear whatever would make you feel good. You do not have to keep up with fashion fads and trends; only

wear what makes you feel confident, comfortable, and happy.

*D*o Not be afraid to let go of toxic people and relationships.

Not everyone takes responsibility for the kind of energy they put out into the world. If there is anyone who adds negativity or toxicity to your life and will not take responsibility for it, it means you need to get away from them. Do not be afraid to let them go. It is vital and liberating, even though it may be painful at first.

Remember that you must be watchful and protective of your energy. It is not prideful or wrong to remove yourself from situations or stay away from people who drain your energy.

*a*nalyze your fears.

Like making mistakes, being scared is natural. Do not dismiss your fears; instead, try to understand them. This healthy exercise will be beneficial to your mental health. Cross-examining and assessing your worries will help you gain clarity and unravel issues in your life that were giving you anxiety. That, in turn, will help ease some, if not all, of your fear.

. . .

*B*elieve in your ability to make good decisions for yourself.

We are so quick to doubt ourselves and our ability to do the right thing, when most of the time, we know in our hearts what is best for us. Keep in mind that your feelings are valid. You are not losing touch with reality. You know yourself longer than anyone else, so be your best supporter.

*U*se every opportunity life brings to you or create your own.

If you keep waiting for the perfect time to take the next step in your life, it will never come. The circumstances may not be ideal, but they should not stop you from achieving your dreams and goals. Instead, take charge of the moment because it may never come back.

*L*earn to Put yourself first.

It is easy to feel guilty about putting yourself first, but there is no reason to feel that way. Women can get used to putting others first. Even though there is a time and a place for this, it should not become a habit that robs you of your mental or emotional well-being. Take out time to decompress. When you do not relax or recharge, you can place a lot of strain on yourself. Whether it is spending some extra hours in bed or spending time in the outdoors, find out what helps you decompress and dedicate time for yourself.

*A*llow yourself to feel pain and joy.
Let yourself feel everything fully. Lean into pain, be happy in your joy, and do not put a limit on your feelings. Just as fear, pain, and joy are emotions that can help you understand yourself, you will eventually realize that you are not your feelings.

*D*o Not be afraid to assert yourself in public.
Make a habit of speaking your mind. Practicing boldness is like exercising a muscle — it grows the more you use it. Do not wait for permission to sit at the table or join a conversation. Do not be afraid to contribute your thoughts. Act and know that your views and opinions are just as important as anyone else's.

*L*earn to appreciate the beauty in simple things.
Learn to be observant of at least one small, the beautiful thing around you every day. Could you take note of it and be grateful for it? Gratitude doesn't just give your perspective; it also helps you stay joyful.

Learn to show yourself kindness.

The world is full of cruel words and critics; do not include yours. Speak kind words to yourself, and never call yourself mean names. Learn how to celebrate yourself. You've come so far and have grown so much. Don't wait to celebrate for your birthday to celebrate yourself!

*E*ven if you are not feeling particularly powerful, reflect on how far you have come and how much you have been through. You are a survivor. You are here, alive and powerful beyond your imagination. Be patient with yourself. You will not develop self-love overnight, but with time, you will get used to it. You may struggle with it but keep going, and one day you will see how these small steps contributed to making you the best version of yourself.

～

CHAPTER 2
TOXIC BEHAVIOR AWARENESS

*T*oxic relationships always cause severe damage to people, workplaces, and families. But weak and insecure people are not the only ones who can find themselves in unhealthy relationships. Strong and independent people can also get entangled in the grip of a toxic relationship or marriage. Likewise, relationships that start very well with the couple being madly in love can again descend into the ashes of separation and a nasty divorce.

People, relationships grow and evolve. Things change as time goes on, and sometimes we begin to see things we never thought we would in our Relationships. Truthfully, we can never fully know a person no matter how long we live with them because people change and grow. And sometimes, those changes are unpleasant. We can never tell how anything will turn out when we start to discover each other's less attractive and awful habits. These habits are often hidden and may never show up except in public, around in-laws, or under the influence of alcohol.

Some relationships start very wrong, with all sorts of red flags showing up in different ways. Ever been on a first date with a man, and he tells you just how much you look like his ex, then proceeds to show you thousands of pictures of her on his phone, laptop, and other digital gadgets? That's a major red flag right there. Some other relationships start with so much promise, but things start to fall apart along the way. All the good and beautiful things get replaced with hurt, cruelty, jealousy, obsessiveness, and resentment.

Love is a beautiful thing, and we all love the euphoria that comes with being in love, but our hearts can sometimes lead us astray. While we follow our hearts into what we believe to be a relationship made in heaven, we end up in a toxic relationship that we cannot leave. The search for true love can blind us that we never realize how far we have gone until we're so deep into it. Worse still, you may never find out that something was not right until you are three kids and a mortgage into the relationship before finding out that you have lost yourself.

*W*hat is a toxic relationship?
A toxic relationship hurts your self-esteem, steals your happiness, and alters how you see yourself and the world. A toxic person usually goes through life with a trail of broken hearts, broken rela-

tionships, and broken people behind them. Still, unhealthy relationships are not necessarily a direct result of dating a toxic person. Sometimes relationships start on a good note until negative feelings, bad history, or unrealized expectations enter and change the people involved. Sometimes, it takes time, but other times, it can happen so fast. And yes, it can happen to strong and independent people.

*I*s it worth fighting for?
Every relationship is worth fighting for, but there is a point you get to where you have to give up. In a toxic relationship, there will be problems: mood swings, anger, unhappiness. Sometimes, you may even have to stay away from each other more. Your work and relationships outside the toxic relationship may begin to suffer.

When a relationship is toxic, all the fights in the world will not change anything because one or both partners have emotionally moved on. Sometimes, they were never really there in the first place, or not in the way you thought they were or needed them to be anyway. What is even worse is that if your relationship is toxic, you will be more and more damaged by staying and trying to "fight" for yourself. Struggling to hold on to something that is not struggling to hold on to you, will destroy you. Sometimes you must let go. Move on with your life.

Are people born with toxic traits, or are they

learned? How do you identify harmful characteristics in men? Unhealthy behaviors can show up in people from a very young age. Sometimes, these behaviors are coping mechanisms to deal with a form of abuse. When a young boy is growing up in a dysfunctional home, his mind will formulate various coping mechanisms to protect himself from his harmful environment. But the problem lies when those coping mechanisms become so ingrained in his mind, and he fails to unlearn them when he becomes an adult. They become toxic traits, and if he does not realize how harmful these traits are, his children are likely to learn those traits from him. The people who are most affected by toxic marriages are children. It is a vicious cycle that only ends when one or both partners decide to put a stop to it.

The Twelve Pillars of Toxic Behavior

We know how poisonous being in a toxic relationship can be. For some reason, it seems like all toxic people dust us with their poison. Sometimes it is more like a drenching. For some reason that science is yet to explain, opposites tend to attract. Difficult people find themselves drawn to the calm and reserved ones, and all of us have been in a relationship with at least one person who has had us bent around ourselves like barbed wire, all in a bid to please them. Unfortunately, we can never please such people.

Toxicity is so dangerous because of how subtle it is.

Many toxic men are not violent, but the mind games they play are just as damaging. Their go-to tactic is the 'It is not them, it is me" game. They will make you seem like you are over-reacting, being oversensitive, or tend to misinterpret things. If you are the one who is always on the receiving end of the one who constantly changes to please them to avoid getting hurt, then you have to realize that it has nothing to do with you. It is entirely their fault.

Being able to identify their harmful behavior is the first step to reducing their impact. You may not have the power to change what your partner does, but you can change how you react to what he does. You can also change any idea that that toxic man in your life might have that he can get away with his behavior. There are many things toxic men do to manipulate their partners and situations to their advantage.

These Twelve behaviors are the central pillars of toxic traits. Knowing then will prevent you from becoming a victim of their influence.

1. He will make you constantly wonder which version of them you are getting.

If you are in a toxic relationship or have ever been in one, you will be familiar with the constant state of panic and fear you experience all the time. One day, he will be delighted, and the next, you will be wondering what you did to upset your partner so much. The scary thing is that there usually is not anything obvious that will explain their change of attitude. All you know is that your gut tells you that something is wrong. Sometimes, they will give you subtle hints that something is wrong. Such hints could be a heavy sigh or raised brow, or a cold shoulder.

When things like these happen, you find yourself making excuses for him or trying your best to make him happy. Do you see how manipulative it is? They're causing you to break your backs to please them without even saying anything.

So how do you respond to such behavior? Do not try to please them. Toxic men know that their partners will go to any length to see them happy. If you do your best to please them and it does not work, you have to stop. It will be difficult, but it starts with a "no."

When he begins to have his mood swings, walk away. Leave that environment and come back when he's in a better mood. Unlike what many women in toxic relationships think, you are not responsible for his feelings. But if you believe that you may have done something wrong to him, apologize sincerely. But it would be best if you didn't have to guess all the time.

2. He Will Manipulate You All of the Time.

If you feel like you are the only one trying to make the relationship work, you are in a toxic relationship. Toxic men always try to make you feel as though you owe them something. They are very entitled. They will always want to hurt you and take from you, all the while making you believe that they are doing it for your benefit. This behavior is prevalent in relationships where the balance of power is being abused or entirely ignored. You do not owe anybody anything.

You do not owe your husband or your partner anything except to love and respect them. If, at any point in time, you believe that what they're calling a favor does not feel like a favor, then it isn't.

3. He Will Not Even Acknowledge Your Feelings.

Rather than acknowledging their feelings, he will act as if those feelings are yours. It is called projection in psychology. They will transfer their feelings and thoughts to you. For instance, instead of your man telling you that he is angry, he will accuse you of being mad at him. You must have experienced this during an argument with him. And it can be as subtle as him asking 'Are you okay with me?' or a bit more direct, 'Why are you angry at me,' or 'You have been in a bad mood all day.'

Before you know it, you will find yourself justifying and defending your feelings and thoughts. It will go on and on in a never-ending circle because it was never about you in the first place. Be clear about what you are feeling and what you are not. Do not accept their feelings as your own. If you feel the constant need to defend yourself many times or answer questions that do not add up, he may project his feelings onto you. Do not assume that you have to respond to baseless accusations. Never forget that.

3. He Will Want You to Prove Yourself to Him Constantly.

Toxic men will always make you feel like you are never enough. They will keep you in a position where you have to choose between them and someone or something else. And in those times, you will feel an obligation to choose them.

Sometimes they will wait until you have an essential commitment or a promise to fulfill before starting their drama. They will say something like, 'If you cared about me, you'd skip your book club and spend time with me.' The problem with this is that nothing you do will ever be enough. There is no satisfying these people. Do not be coerced into giving up the things you love to please him. You have a life, too, and you owe it to yourself to live it to the fullest and achieve your dreams.

4. He Will Never Apologize.

Toxic men will lie a thousand times over before they ever apologize, so it does not help argue with them. They will alter the story to their advantage, change the way it happened and retell it so convincingly that they will believe their lie. People must not apologize to be wrong. You do not even need an apology to move on. You only have to take that step.

Please do not give up your truth to make him feel good or to continue arguing, and there's no need for that. Sometimes, people care more about being correct than being happy. Do not feed the flames by keeping up the argument or trying to prove that you're right.

6. He Will Never Share in Your Happiness and Achievements.

If you are dating a toxic man or married to one, you must have experienced this several times. Something extraordinary happens to you, and you're celebrating, but then he makes you look stupid for being happy. Let's say you got promoted at work and you are pleased about it, 'The money is not a big deal for the amount of work you will be doing.' Or you just got the opportunity to go for a holiday, and he says, 'Well, it gets scorching there. Do you still want to go?' Do you see the pattern? Toxic people can be found everywhere, especially in the workplace, but we are focusing on toxic men for the sake of this book. Don't let him ruin your happiness or reduce your sense of self. Don't ever second-guess yourself because of him.

7. He Will leave in the middle of a conversation and then go off the radar.

Here this usually happens when you're having a chat with him. He'll leave in the middle of the conversation without warning. He will not pick up his calls or reply to text messages and emails. In between the tons of voicemails, you leave him, and you'll find yourself thinking about the status of your relationship. You will begin to play the conversation over and over again in your head. You'll almost work yourself into a frenzy thinking about what you did to upset him and why he is ignoring you. Someone who genuinely cares about your feelings will not let you get so worked up with worry over nothing. If there is a problem, your partner will try to sort it out with you. Leaving you during a serious conversation is a toxic trait that you must have in mind.

8. He knows how to use non-toxic expressions with a toxic tone.

The words he uses might seem innocent, but his tone will convey something else. Take a seemingly harmless question like, 'What did you do today?' It seems pretty straightforward, but it can mean many things depending on how he says it for a toxic man. It could mean 'So I guess you did nothing – as always' or 'I'm sure your day was better than mine. Mine was horrible. And you didn't even notice.' When you question his tone, he'll say something like, 'But I only asked what you did today." You shouldn't constantly have to guess what he's saying if he is sincere about his feelings.

9. He'll bring up irrelevant details into a conversation.

Whenever you're trying to settle an important issue, he will bring up something that has nothing to do with the present problem. Sometimes he may even talk about something you both argued about two weeks ago. When this happens, you'll abandon the current issue and begin to rehash something that you both talked about several weeks or months ago. Whenever you speak to him, the conversation shifts to something wrong that you did to him.

10. He will concentrate on the way you're speaking instead of the problem at hand.

You are probably trying to resolve an issue or get clarification. After a while, the conversation takes another turn. This guy ignores the issue that is important to you and focuses on how you talked about it. He doesn't mind if there is a problem with your manners or not. You'll begin to defend your tone, gestures, and words– it doesn't always have to make sense. That man will often combine your needs with the pile of unfinished conversations that seem to grow larger every day.

11. He embellishes.

You are probably used to the phrases, 'You always ...' 'You never ...'. Over time, it gets more challenging to defend yourself against this type of manipulation. Toxic men have a way of harping on the one time you didn't do something or the one time you did to accuse you. Don't entangle yourself in such arguments. You won't win, and there's no need to succeed.

12. He is judgmental to the third degree.

We all make mistakes sometimes, but a toxic man will make sure you know it. He'll judge you and poke at your self-esteem, making you believe that you're less because you made a mistake. We're all allowed to get it wrong from time to time, and we're all human no one has the right to judge you.

*N*ow that you know the twelve central pillars of toxic behavior, it will make it easier for you to avoid getting in unhealthy relationships if you are single or divorced. It will also help you to deal with these behaviors if you are in an unhealthy relationship. It is the first step to breaking free. Some people will never be satisfied no matter how much you try to please them. Doing that only drives you deeper into their hold until you lose yourself completely. Be confident and accept your strengths and weaknesses. Accept your quirks and the things that make you shine.

Toxic behavior in men is encouraged by toxic masculinity. In the next chapter, I'll discuss toxic masculinity and how it affects the family and society.

CHAPTER 3
MASCULINITY VS. TOXIC MASCULINITY

*T*oxic masculinity is a phrase frequently used to refer to negative male attributes. The term has developed over many years and now has a place in the scholarly world and regular discourse. Constant use of the expression causes certain people to misunderstand what toxic masculinity is. The traditional concept of masculinity is complex. Some people believe it is difficult and move past these negative ideas about male attributes.

Masculinity and manliness are not the same.

Masculinity is the result of our hormones and the composition of our brains. The hormones and physiological design create the tendencies for aggression and violence.

Manliness is the ability to use masculinity in a way that will create effective outcomes for everybody involved. Very masculine men are likely to have higher levels of testosterone and vasopressin.

Manliness is about using the tools we do have – physiology, hormones, experience, beliefs, etc. – to produce the outcomes we need; this is manliness.

Femininity can be incorporated smoothly, transitioning it to be a match for the manly and masculine, and Femininity is nurturing, kindness, empathy, compassion, and love. These are qualities a man can exhibit, as well. They are not exclusive to women, as masculine virtues are not exclusive to men. And there are times where men should tap into feminine energy and power.

*W*hat is toxic masculinity?
The precise meaning of toxic masculinity has developed over time. A study conducted published by the Journal of School of Psychology defines toxic masculinity as: "the group of socially regressive [masculine] traits that promote domination, the devaluation of women, homophobia, and wanton violence."

In present-day culture, people frequently use the term toxic masculinity to refer to exaggerated manly attributes that numerous societies have generally accepted and celebrated.

*T*his dangerous concept of masculinity puts critical significance on 'manliness' based on:

- Strength
- Lack Of Emotion
- Independence
- Dominance
- Sexual Virility

As indicated by conventional toxic masculine qualities, a man who doesn't show enough of these attributes cannot be considered a 'real man.' The exaggeration of these attributes may lead to dangerous tendencies in somebody attempting to reach these expectations. **Some harmful trends are:**

- Aggression
- Sexual Aggression Or Control
- Showing No Feeling Or Smothering One's Feelings
- Hyper-Competitiveness
- A Desire To Rule Or Control Others
- An Inclination Towards Or Glorification Of Viciousness.
- Isolation
- Low Compassion
- Entitlement
- Chauvinism And Sexism

An example of this is telling a man who shows some emotion to "man up" or hide his feelings. This example shows how a few groups see emotion or weakness as 'unmanly.' Another instance is the cliche "boys will be boys." This statement supports thoughtless, violent, and harming conduct in young men instead of showing them duty and taking responsibility for their slip-ups.

Expressions of this kind show how societies have generally perceived men. Nevertheless, these perspectives can cause harm and embellish the idea of masculinity, leading to a more toxic disposition toward these practices.

*T*he origin of toxic masculinity.
The term toxic masculinity comes from the Mythopoetic Men's Development during the 1980s. This development, established by men for men, served as an outlet for men to express their 'manliness.' Certain groups of men felt they were not free to express these generally male or manly practices in an advanced society that considered them to be harmful.

People from the group accepted that they would be chauvinistic or hateful toward women if they could not express these male attributes.

As characterized by the Mythopoetic Men's Development, this unique idea of toxic masculinity has always been criticized. This was because it proposed that masculinity has one unadulterated structure, which is not the situation.

Numerous people currently see masculinity as a mix of practices formed by different elements, including:

- Age

- Race
- Class
- Culture
- Sexuality
- Religion

Accordingly, what characterizes masculinity can take various structures. What one society or even subculture sees as manly, another may dismiss. Masculinity, at that point, turns into a comforting thought as opposed to a complex, limited arrangement of rules.

Traditional masculinity

The underlying foundations of what numerous people see as masculinity -were created when early homo sapiens used strength, for instance, to apply predominance or assume responsibility. The best male homo sapiens were the people who could battle and chase. On those occasions, the best attributes would almost certainly have included hostility, heartlessness, and actual strength.

These practices proceeded for quite a long time. From the beginning of time, predominant male rulers have acquired force by defeating others. This example stayed unaltered until the 1980s and 1990s, when these customary male practices got contradictory with the perspectives on contemporary society.

Be that as it may, because contemporary society has prompted such a move in demeanor toward these male practices. Because it no longer praises these old perspectives on masculinity, specific groups subcultures succumb to these 'normal standards.' This is when masculinity can become 'toxic.' It is this requirement for particular men to be a sure route as directed by a philosophy that has been old since quite a while ago.

On the off chance that a male accepts they are not gathering these misrepresented qualities or not lining up with these thin perspectives, they may feel they are missing the mark. It may bring about a need to lash out or overstate these attributes to restore their 'masculinity.' This lashing out can prompt truly perilous conduct, both to the individual or people around them.

While a few groups use the term toxic masculinity to include every manly quality, this may be an approach to put down all guys, not simply these masculine attributes.

From an honest perspective, masculinity itself is not toxic. It is those negative attributes that are ascribed to men and permitted by a society that it so.

Effects of toxic masculinity

A few groups accept that toxic masculinity is dangerous because it restricts an individual's development and contorts the true meaning of being a man. It puts a strain on a man who does not seem to meet up with society's expectations of him.

When a kid or adult male perspective sees the world through society's twisted lens, they believe that people will accept them if they meet those expectations.

Unchecked Toxic Masculinity Can Lead To Various Problems In Society, Such As:

- Harassment And Maltreatment Of Women
- Indiscipline
- Academic Difficulties
- Prison Or Jail Time
- Abusive Behavior At Home
- Rape
- Substance Abuse
- Self-Destructive Behavior
- Mental Disorders
- Inability To Form A Friendship.

Some theories have shown that toxic masculinity plays a role in affecting a man's well-being. Toxic masculinity may prevent a few men from seeking help for potential medical problems and other likely issues. For confident guys, requesting help may trigger feelings of deficiency, weakness, or a sense of being 'less than a man.'

How does it affect mental health?

Toxic masculinity can negatively affect a man who does not meet these expectations but feels compelled to do so. The American Psychological Association observes the risks of attempting to stick to these overstated manly qualities. Men obligated to adhere to these attributes regularly experience the negative impacts of this and begin to have several problems ranging from:

- Discouragement
- Identity Issues
- Substance Abuse
- Stress

Since talking about their emotions conflicts with these conservative manly qualities, men who have mental health issues will not discuss it with their families or seek help.

How to Fight Toxic Masculinity – breaking out of the man-box

So how do we eliminate the man-box and make men understand that they don't have to be mean or cruel to be called men? Here are a few strategies we can use to fight toxic masculinity.

1. Create awareness

In a research published in the journal titled "Gender Roles," Scientists asked a group of male undergrads to talk about ladies' perception. Many of them repeated some false perspectives society has promoted about women, such as, "Ladies are easily angered" or "Ladies are generally sweet until they've gotten a man, yet then they reveal who they are." Next, Scientists told the men to talk about their perceptions of the average man."

Other studies like this have discovered that men

reliably overestimate the sexism of different men. They participate in pluralistic obliviousness, which is the suspicion that their perspectives are in the minority when indeed they're in the majority.

Due to misogynist mentalities, if a man accepts that his circle has men who are more chauvinist than he will be, such a man will be less inclined to speak out when he observes chauvinist conduct. He will be bound to quietly and awkwardly return the high-five his amigo offers. The result? Pluralistic obliviousness gets built up.

After the polls, many men got no criticism. The remaining were told about the inconsistencies in their report and counseled on the proper mindset. In three weeks, the men retook the surveys, and the scientists had a clearer perspective on where most men stood.

As indicated by this study, changing mindsets is possible. It could reduce chauvinist tendencies, curtail inappropriate behavior, rude jokes, etc.

2. Be vocal about quitting the man-box.

Men who need the most assistance are usually the least likely to seek it. However, a group of studies showed that when men saw that their male companions and family members sought help, they were bound to do likewise. Driving under the influence or smoking has recorded the same results. When men see this acceptance of vulnerability and openness towards other men, it helps them become better men, allowing them to be open.

It's important to be vocal about quitting. When a

man rejects these stereotypes, he sets the pace for other men to follow, especially those who need help the most.

3. Any action is masculine if a man is enthusiastic about it.

While there's nothing wrong with wanting to mow the lawn after watching a romantic comedy, it's an indication that some activities are perceived to be for real men. Toxic masculinity takes it a step further by stating that some actions are masculine while others are not.

Doing something that is not "traditionally accepted" to be for men pushes men to reflect on masculinity. It is a good way of helping men to leave the man-box.

For instance, a study conducted in Taiwan studied the connection between manly exercises and caffeinated drinks. Caffeinated drinks with names like Venom, Full Throttle, and Bawls, media-focused caffeinated drinks on young men who wanted to become more masculine.

In the survey, about 100 male students took a poll about their favorite exercises, which were all purposely sexually impartial, such as going on Facebook, voyaging, and drinking espresso. Then, the men were given one of three results: The poll told them that their picks scored either high on masculinity, low on masculinity, or ranked somewhere in the middle. It also criticized them based on their choices.

At that point, each man participated in a caffeinated drink trial. They were given two distinctive caffeinated flavors and asked to drink as much as they wanted. The men whose choices have been criticized for not being masculine enough drank more than those whose intentions were applauded or left alone.

In this particular study, these stereotypes' effect was not too damaging but think about what happens in real-life situations. Horrible events such as mass shootings, aggressive behavior at home, and other harmful behaviors are employed by men to asserts their masculinity.

*D*o not accept the general concept of masculine versus non-masculine exercises and instruct young men that any movement they are energetic about is "man enough." And on the off chance that they want to certify their masculinity, urge them to do it in manners that develop themselves without destroying others.

4. Encourage Multiple Roles and Relationships.

Since toxic masculinity says men are not permitted to have close friendships with anybody other than a spouse, they put every one of their eggs in a single relationship basket. Moreover, toxic masculinity restricts a man to what he does, which implies that his work regularly turns into his personality. When he deals with unemployment, his entire world crumbles around him.

Yet, when men achieve success in their jobs, everybody benefits. Children who spend time with their fathers and get encouragement from them have lower risks of engaging in harmful activities, and they are less likely to have depression and live a full life. Everybody wins when men create solid bonds with family, friends, and society.

Toxic masculinity negatively affects everyone. Encourage a broad scope of jobs and connections for all men. Everybody will profit from it.

~

CHAPTER 4

TOXIC REINDEER GAMES

*a*t a certain point in Shakespeare's Hamlet, the writer has Hamlet say to Guildenstern, "Why, look you now, how dishonorable a thing you make of me! You would play upon me, and you would appear to know my stops. You would cull out the core of my secret."

Shakespeare was discussing control and playing with someone's mind to get something from them without knowing it. People have been playing mind games from the beginning of time.

We play mind games with each other because it makes us feel powerful and frees us from taking responsibility for our actions. But the dangerous thing about mind games is that you will never have a real connection with people. You will never experience the feeling of genuineness and trust in a healthy relationship.

. . .

*I*n human relationships, especially romantic relationships, toxic men love to play mind games with their partners. Some of them are innocent, while others are not. You must be careful to discern the difference between harmless games and those that seek to undermine you.

Here is a list of some familiar mind games that men play:

1. Disqualification.

Disqualification is a technique for saying something harmful to somebody, and afterward, when they become hurt, doing a one-two punch by causing it to appear, you did not at all mean what they thought you implied.

You may say to somebody, "In some cases, you are not kidding." If the individual gets hurt (which you intentionally or unknowingly need), you answer, "Goodness, and I was kidding. Here and there, you're so over-delicate." Not just do you hurt them once, yet you damage them twice by excluding what you initially said and afterward offending them. Men who use this technique can drive the other individual, both mad and befuddled.

2. Forgetting.

Detached forceful characters play this game. Essentially, they fail to remember important things like arrangements, guarantees, taking care of credit, and so forth. You hang tight for them to recall; however, they do not, and when you bring it up, they answer, "Goodness, I'm so sorry, I forgot."

After bringing it up a few times, you begin to get irritated. At that point, they say, "Oh, and I'm truly sorry. Is it safe to say that you are angry? You appear to be irate."

If *you* inquire as to whether they are angry at *you*, they fight, "Gracious, God no. If I were, I'd tell you." They drive you to feel that you're crazy over nothing, which causes you to get angrier. The forgetting trait is how they "dump" their resentment onto you without voicing your anger.

3.Persecuting.

At times people project their scorn onto others and abuse them. They are ignorant of their hatred, or they believe it is justified. When people start anticipating, they search for motivations to abuse.

If the hated people cannot help contradicting them on legislative issues, turn a greeting, or grin the incorrect way, the persecutor figures out how to check them. They may ridicule them behind their backs, get others to group face them, or address them in a deigning or offending way. They judge them as awful or cruel and treat them likewise. They never examine their emotions or attempt to work things out. It is something contrary to the brilliant guideline, "Do unto others as you would have them do unto you." This could be expressed, "Cross others for not being what you need them to be."

4. Guilt-Tripping.

The game here is to cause somebody to feel remorseful except if they do what you need them to do. A spouse considers her better half a "misogynist."

From the outset, he may dissent, however ultimately, altogether not to be a chauvinist, and he attempts to be the sort of husband she needs.

A spouse tells his significant other she is bone-chilling since he needs her to feel regretful about not having intercourse with him.

5. Gaslighting.

The expression "gaslighting" comes from the excellent film with Ingrid Bergman, in which her better half attempts to make her believe she is going off the deep end since she sees things (for example, the gas lights going on and off). When she sees the lights going on and off, he says *he does not see that* by any means.

Some troubled people use this procedure on a disliked relative. They say and get things done and afterward deny that at any point told them.

At that point, when their partner continues raising these things, the Gaslighter starts to scrutinize the other's mental stability. "I think perhaps you have an over-dynamic creative mind, my dear." At the time, the upset individual isn't even conscious the person is doing it.

6. Shaming.

People who play this disgracing game express their anger by hoping to get to people they do not care for by saying or accomplishing something they think is inappropriate.

It is something contrary to romanticizing some-body; it is slandering somebody. A strict aggressor individual may sit tight for the people who are not strict to say, "some unacceptable thing."

"Religion is not in every case great," somebody may say. The tough nut may then hop on them as they would a beast, disseminate their statement everywhere on the web in a shocked tone, and request an expression of remorse. This game empowers the *Shamer* to dump their outrage while looking to the world like a guiltless, concerned resident.

7. Pretending.

Pretending can take different structures. A man can profess to be keen on a woman *to get laid*. A Woman can claim to pull a man to *lead him on*, but this would carrying on outrage. People can pretend they are not irate when truth be told, they are furious. People can profess to be your dearest companion to get you to believe them while they conceal their natural thought processes.

Great fakers are acceptable entertainers. Once in a while, they even persuade themselves that they are earnest. In therapy, we call that a response development. An individual might be envious of you, yet deny it to himself and persuade himself regarding the inverse that he wishes the best for you. On the off chance that you accept such an individual, you may fall into their snare and not think twice about it. Pretending is a method of controlling you are dodging any showdown that may result from trustworthiness.

These psyche games are terrible enough when they happen among grown-ups, yet lamentably a few guardians accidentally play these games with their youngsters, leaving them hurt and puzzled. These games all have benefits, yet they prevent real emotions from forming, which is what makes every day worth experiencing. Avoid the people who play these games and lean towards the people who do not.

Dating mind games

#1. The Bait and Switch Game

At that point, the lure is showing interest first, exchanging with (counterfeit) lack of engagement. Not gladly, I have been doing it without anyone's help a couple of times as of late. Not actually to play dating mind games, but since I am driven and occupied with my stuff. Furthermore, I lose interest on the off chance that I do not see responded interest or potential if the principal date is not sufficiently hot to make our darlings. In any case, a few men may use this one on you with an end goal to make you pursue.

Here is what it looks like:

Men will play this game frequently when they are exceptionally occupied on their primary goal when they are just somewhat intrigued or have a few ladies that involve their time (or a rotation of multiple women).

He makes some great memories with you yet never calls you back, showing you that he does not care for you. That distance drives you to think about him endlessly, which sucks you deeper into his trap.

How to Handle It:

Please do not believe anything is real until it is actual, and words are rarely sincere. Focus on the man's actions. Also, work on your self-esteem. These games consistently work best on people with poor self-esteem.

#2. The Adventurer Game

The Adventurer is a notorious dating game. He introduces himself as a globe-trotter, Adventurer, or God's gift to women. He makes you believe that he is so hot that women constantly flock around him.

Men use this tactic to trick ladies into giving up their "cookies." For this reason, ladies are advised not to have sex with a man they just started dating. Most ladies will head straight to bed if they believe that he is unavailable.

It is nothing but an ill-conceived notion designed to get you into his bed. Don't fall for it!

How to Handle It:

Whenever a guy introduces himself as a Ladies' man or Adventurer, simply laugh in his face. But if you want to go further, tell him something like this:

"You are like the tenth person who has told me this in the last two days. I believe it is shaky for a man to try so hard on the first date." Observe how fast a pricked ego can deflate.

#3. The "I Never Date THIS type" game.

Which is similar to the "disqualifier." He makes you think that you are not good enough for him and that he will not come after you. He wants to arouse your curiosity and make you the pursuer.

So, If you are a brunette, he may say something like, "I only date blondes," or if you're white, he may say, "Sorry, but I prefer black women."

It works because people tend to desire what they cannot have. He will maintain contact with you to give you the illusion that you can have him, but he'll never come after you.

How to Handle It:

The trick is to do the same thing to him. So, when he says that he prefers blondes, you can say something like, "Oh really, but blondes prefer blonde men too. Do you think you can find a blonde woman who'll be attracted to you?"

Try NOT to sound mean. It would be best if you said it as if you are anxious for him. As if to say, "Poor you, can you truly find any of these young ladies that you prefer?".

He will be lost for a few moments and may try to bounce back by convincing you that he can. But the tables have turned, and he is trying to prove himself to you.

#4. The Chameleon Game (AKA: "We're So Alike")

The sexual chameleon does what a chameleon does: He adapts. The sexual chameleon fakes interest in the things you like and tries to be very much like the person you dream to date. If your ex were a toxic man, the chameleon would come across as caring and steady. If your ex were a more caring, eager to please person, the chameleon would act aloof and disinterested.

How to Handle It:

Do not believe everything he shows you. If you fall for him, you will lose yourself in that relationship. Instead, do not conclude until you see solid verifications of his behavior. Try to confuse him. If you mention some qualities about your ex and constantly try to prove that he's the opposite, call him out on it and see how he reacts.

#4.2. The "I Like What You Like" Game

Another version of this trick is to introduce himself in a way that will make you believe you both share similar interests.

#5. The "My Girlfriend" Game

The "My Girlfriend" Game is dangerous, especially for ladies desperately looking for a relationship. What is more important, it is usually gets used against ladies who have decided to "make him hang tight for sex."

So what does this man do? He will try to give you what you want as fast as possible to get what he wants. He wants sex, and you want a relationship. So, he will put a label on you. He will call you his girlfriend or even his wife.

The trick is to make you believe that you can safely have sex with him since you are both officially an item. Not all men will vanish after sex, and not all men play this game with malignancy. So do not get angry with him if he calls you his sweetheart before sex. He may not have such intentions.

Nonetheless, it is a possibility you ought to consider.

Search for indications of trickiness, an absence of past relationships, and an example of lies, as little, they may be.

How to Handle It:

Say that you would lean toward not utilizing marks until it is true and commonly concurred that both of you are together. Try not to say it in a meaningful method, obviously, and the more you like him, the hotter you need to be with your conveyance. Also, ensure you do it secretly as anything comparable openly would be a significant shame for him.

#6. The "I Can Help You" Game

Numerous men who listen to dating advice will not play this one since they fear contributing too much to the relationship too soon, just like most ladies, after all. However, more intelligent men realize that offering assistance is amazingly charming and alluring - after all, only men with good connections, social skills, and assets can offer service. Likewise, there is an incredible, subliminal impact where you feel that to "completely offer" that proposal of help, you may need to give him something first.

Since you most likely don't have any associations or information that he doesn't have now. Gosh, would it be that he trusts you will give him? Your body.

How to Handle It:

Once more, words are just as meaningless as air contamination in Beijing. Allow him to think of all the possibilities he can imagine and tell him, "Thank you so much. I'd love to meet this incredible person you keep talking about. When will you introduce us?" Do not contact him again until he makes that introduction.

#7. Game of Chicken

Games of chicken are power games to get an advantage in the relationship. Games of chicken take steps to cut down the entire relationship except if she obeys, contributes, or pursues. When she disintegrates and ultimately finishes, she submits and gives him the reins of the relationship - or, in any event, more force.

In a serious relationship, trying to avoid him is a type of chicken game (though women play that frequently). Right off the bat in dating, not answering your calls can be a round of chicken.

How to Handle It:

Pay close attention to his behaviors that detect if he is either avoiding you or ignoring you to get his way. Do not avoid him; it will only make matters worst. Stand firm on your boundaries and beliefs, allow him to know that a mutual understanding is needed and that he cannot keep running away from the issue.

#8. The Casually Planned Date Game

The Casually Planned Date Game is not in the class of "horrible mind games," yet you must be wary of it. He will casually plan a date to make you believe that you are both just having fun and getting to know each other. However, he intends to make you have sex with him or sell the idea to you.

How to Handle It

Usually, he will carefully arrange his house in a way that will entice you to have sex with him. Do not fall for it. Take note of those subtle hints at sex and do not even think of spending the night at his place.

A man who does not play games will either come out and say there isn't anything wrong. Or he might say something like, "well, isn't this my job to make you comfortable in my house? I want to have good memories with you. You're the first lady I'm bringing to my home."

#9. "Excellence is Common" Game

He is attempting to paint himself as both experienced, profound, and inspired by your character. Perhaps you bother him. He is just searching for sex. He will make you believe that excellence is standard and that he is searching for something more profound.

Both tactics work in his favor. He will make you think he is highly sought after by many ladies. He will also make you believe that he can value you for who you are apart from your attractive physical attributes (giant boobs, glossy hair, and so forth)

This tactic will work on many ladies. You have to realize that he still wants to have sex with you at the back of his mind regardless of whatever stellar qualities you have.

How to Handle It:

Ladies will, in general, accept this game not because they are simple but because they think that only a few men feel this way. But honestly, 95% of men will tell you whatever you want to hear. All they want is to have sex with you.

On the other 4% of the occasions, the person has been around so much and has a certain standard. In 1% of the cases, you may have discovered genuine gold. It is rare, but men like that do exist.

#9.2. The "Incomparable Sex god."

Another trick is to go straight for the sexual and make himself look like a sexual God, promising unforgettable sex, climaxes, and a mind-blowing experience. He will do everything to convince you that he will blow your mind in bed.

This game's best players do it brazenly, with stories, sexual innuendo, and non-verbal communication.

Do not hesitate to go for this one, even if that is what you are looking for. See it for what it is, a game.

*H*ere is a list of more violent games that men play. These games eat away at your self-esteem and undermine your sense of self-worth.

Bringing down Your Self Esteem Games

Why would a man deliberately want you to feel bad about who you are or try to poke at your self-esteem? The answer is that it gives them power over you. Remember what we discussed earlier about toxic behaviors? The goal is to twist your perception of yourself and even make you dependent on them, and they plan to bring down the lady's confidence and make her pursue him. Sadly, they usually succeed in their goals.

There are many ways he can do this to you. Some of them are pretty obvious, while others are very subtle. Sometimes, he will emphasize your weaknesses so much whenever you attempt to take a step forward.

Here are some examples:

Let's say you tell him that you want to go to the gym to work out. He may then do something like tugging your lower arm and say, "YOU want to work out?!"

You are eating, and then you say that you *have had enough*. Your partner then puts a hand on your tummy and says, "Sure, you have."

You say you do not care for working out, and he answers, "why not? My ex adored working out. She was so fit."

How to Handle It:

Lowering your self-esteem is perhaps the most treacherous mind game men play, and you should treat it appropriately. Poor self-confidence will make ladies more vulnerable to this game. Harsh men and oppressive men usually play this game. They will make you have a lousy perspective on yourself.

Stop it immediately and call him out on it. It would be best if you spoke out directly. You can say something like this:

"Look, maybe you implied it as a joke, but I do not find it funny anymore. You have done this before, and I ignored it. However, it is the second time you do it, and I am worried that this is a pattern. These kinds of jokes cause people to feel sad and shameful. It is not how good relationships work."

"You would not think it funny if I joked about you being limp or sexually inadequate, right? That is why I want to please stop these jokes because I do not like the way they make me feel about myself."

When you have told him this, watch his reaction. If he does not stop, then end the relationship. He is not the one for you.

#10. The "Fear Games."

The fear game is a variation of the games talked about above. The men aim to instill fear into you and take control of the relationship.

*H*ow does he do this? Usually, he will do one or more of these things:

He will never completely commit to the relationship.

He will flirt with different ladies before you.

He will create love triangles.

He will constantly tell you about his "hot exes."

We have evaluated a couple of famous mind games men play in dating. But there are other popular mind games that you may have come across while dating. They are:

He was exaggerating the depth of his emotions.

Exaggerating the depth of his emotions is a typical

game, and in a Buss review, 71% of men conceded to having misrepresented their feelings to have sex with a lady.

He is trying to make you believe that he is more than he truly is. Here, you will find men who will lease a vehicle or flaunt properties they do not have.

a. The "I'm alpha."

These are the excessively showy eye-catching devices he employs to make you think they are lovely people who have it all. Fast cars, loud sound systems, backslapping with his companions, and trying to get the ladies' attention are all characteristics of the "alpha male."

b. The flatterer

He constantly commends you about your hotness, tastes, or character. But these are signs of flattery. Most times, his words do not hold water.

Typically, it is men who love to sing the praises of other women who use this trick. Be wary as you may be dating a sociopath. Usually, he does this to get something from you.

How to Handle Men Who Play Games

You can handle a man who plays mind games on you, depending on the type of game he plays.

It is true that in the dating world, we all love to mess with each other. We use games to attract people to us and make the relationship enjoyable. But we only do it for fun, and we play violent games on people. Playing subtle games like not answering his calls, playing hard to get, and throwing off signals are all harmless games. Without, dating would be boring.

But it would be best if you only were concerned when these games become Manipulative self-esteem. These tips will help you determine whether a man's games are harmful or not.

If his games are unbiased or add to your self-esteem, you can indulge him. Games are an indication of interest, and it implies he is putting effort into the relationship.

If his games constantly poke at your self-esteem, call him out on it or leave him.

If you choose to stand up to him, his response should determine if he's a keeper or not. If he stops and apologies, then it is a good sign.

If he reduces his games or stops entirely, then you can move on with him.

Harmless Dating Games

Like I mentioned earlier, there are lots of harmless games that men play. These games do not affect your self-esteem or hurt your feelings. They also show that he wants you, and he wants to spice up the relationship.

He mulls over his text messages to make sure he uses the right words. He thinks carefully about the words he tells you.

He carefully schedules your dates and takes the lead in the relationship. He is eager to spend time with you and get to know you better.

Harmless games like this make you want to put effort into the relationship. It also helps you both to form a genuine connection and friendship that will make your relationship strong. Eventually, you both will learn how to communicate effectively and help each other achieve your dreams. This guy may try to impress you by hiding some of his weaknesses at first, but as time goes on, they will be exposed. You will then have to decide if those weaknesses are something that you can put up with.

*D*estructive mind games are extremely harmful.

You cannot get to know who he is because he keeps playing with your mind. Destructive mind games act like a smokescreen that hides other dangerous traits and toxic behaviors that he may have. When these games cease to be delightful, fun, and energetic, they become destructive.

Not all games men play in dating are essentially evil. But it is up to you to identify the destructive game players from the people who use a few positive games to add spice to your relationship.

～

CHAPTER 5

SEX WITH A SOMATIC NARCISSIST HUSBAND

$\mathcal{T}$here's just something about great sex that clouds our judgment and makes us end up in toxic situations. Some women cannot let go of their partners no matter how bad they are treated just because of the great sex. It is understandable: great sex is hard to come by these days. However, a toxic relationship's long-term damage will have on you is far greater than not having good sex for a few years.

In this chapter, I will break down the importance of great sex in a relationship and why many women cannot let go of their partners. I will also share some tips on how to spice up your sexual life for when you finally meet that perfect guy.

Some couple relationships start excellent and become toxic along the line because something has happened in their sex life. If that is the case with you and your partner, you will get your answers in this chapter as well.

. . .

*G*reat Sex, Horrible Marriage

Great sex is a vital part of marriage, but can it salvage a broken relationship? Can great sex turn a toxic husband into a loving, caring partner? Not exactly. You see, sex is often one of the tools that Narcissists use on people. If you are married or dating a narcissist, you will understand this better. So why and how does great sex keep you holding on to your toxic partner?

When it is so obvious that your partner is toxic and steadily damaging your self-esteem, you still find it challenging to let go or leave the relationship because you are impressed with the sex. So what is so fascinating about sex that it makes is take the wrong decisions?

Tunnel Vision

Canadian scientists conducted a study on this topic and published their results in the Archives of Sexual Behavior in 2016. They realized that the need for sex takes away the reasoning of some people because when you are sexually excited, you see with 'tunnel vision.' Sometimes when people are so heated, all they can think about is how to get release. In this context, tunnel vision makes you think about relieving your pent-up sexual tension and nothing else.

At the time, it will not matter that you will need to make the wrong choice to have sex; you will only think about your sexual needs. While Canadian scientists did not include it in their research, it stands to reason that when people have a sexual urge, they would want to satisfy it in the most beautiful way possible. That is why they will not let go of a partner who meets their sexual needs and fantasies yet robs them of all the more critical aspects of a good relationship, such as happiness, excitement, and satisfaction.

Okafor's Law

Another reason why good sex can make people stay connected to those they should be cutting off ties is an interesting concept called 'Okafor's Law.'

Okafor's Law states that: if you have mind-blowing sex with someone once, they become too weak to refuse or resist you from that point forward. Many People believe in Okafor's Law; that is why when you sleep with someone once, and the sex is good, you are likely to do it again.

Great sex is hard to find.

Many women complain about the ignorance of men when it comes to satisfying a women's sexual needs. That is why when a woman who has been having bad sex with previous partners meets someone who rocks her world, she will find it difficult to let him go no matter how toxic he is. Keep this in mind: Good sex is terrific but not more important than your peace.

The quest for toe-curling orgasms

As intoxicating as it is to experience brain-shattering peaks of orgasmic pleasure with a man constantly, it should not stop you from making the right choices. No matter how good or bad the sex is, any relationship that takes away your inner peace, happiness and leaves you incapable of living your dreams and best life is a complete no-no, and you have to go. If he is not good enough for you, you do not need him. Many women are also afraid of what will happen if they leave such a "wonderful" sex partner. But the truth is that you will never know about the other amazing men out there who are waiting to satisfy your sexual and emotional needs? There is a better man out there who will give you better orgasms than what you are getting from your toxic partner.

Narcissists and Sex

Narcissists are dangerous sex partners, and it shows in the bedroom. Sexual narcissists are known to exhibit traits of detachment, violent sexual behavior, and manipulation. Certain behaviors can help you spot a sexual narcissist so that you can avoid them.

What is a sexual narcissist?

Sexual narcissists are highly positive and have an egotistical admiration for their sexual prowess. They can even become consumed by their obsession with sexual performance and people's need to applaud them in the bedroom. Many sexual narcissists have an idealized version of their self-image. They also display a grandiose sense of self-importance.

Although the Diagnostic and Statistical Manual does not categorize the different aspects of narcissism, the Diagnostic and Statistical Manual showed the concept of sexual narcissism in several studies.

According to The Sexual Narcissism Scale, these traits identify a sexual narcissist:

1. Sexual exploitation
2. Sexual entitlement
3. Lack of sexual empathy
4. An exaggerated sense of sexual prowess

*I*n 2013, a study published in the Archives of Sexual Behavior discovered that marriages involving sexual narcissists had lower sexual and marital satisfaction. Some studies have also identified sexual narcissism as a borderline or histrionic personality disorder.

The traits of sexual narcissists

1. Deliberately ignoring you after sex.

A sexual narcissist only cares about their pleasure. They always withdraw from their partner after sex and may never speak with you after that because they have gotten what they wanted. A sexual narcissist can be in a committed relationship or long-term relationship.

Ghosting after sex is common with narcissists. They do not feel the need to contact you after since they have gotten the validation they wanted from the sex. For marriages, narcissists can leave the room or the house after sex. The dangerous thing is that they are always very charming until they get you to have sex. Afterwards, they will ignore and neglect you.

2. They are sexually violent.

Sexual narcissism is associate and with sexual

abuse and aggression. A study printed in the Archives of Sexual Behavior discovered that men with traits of sexual narcissism have tendencies of committing sexual crimes such as unwanted sexual contact, sexual coercion, and even rape.

3. They display compulsive sexual behavior.

Sexual narcissists usually have compulsive behavior when it comes to sex, including unsafe sex and compulsive pornography. It negatively affects their lives as they prefer quantity over quality.

4. They cheat.

One of the compulsions of Sexual narcissists includes serial infidelity. A 2014 research published in the Archives of Sexual Behavior discovered that sexual narcissists tend to cheat in their marriages. And they do so without remorse.

5. They have no empathy for their partners.

Sexual narcissists believe that they own their partners' sexuality and cannot engage in emotional intimacy. A sexual narcissist is solely focused on their pleasure, performance, or any fetishes they may have. They will never ask their partners about their sexual preferences.

For these classes of people, sex has nothing to do with an emotional connection. It's all about self-gratification, dominance, and power.

6. They love to gaslight their partners when they ask for their needs.

Gaslighting is one of the most weapons of a sexual narcissist. They will call you needy when you ask for your needs or ask for an emotional connection. Some of them will even make you believe that you wanted sex when they manipulated you into having it.

7. They use sex as a tool for manipulation.

Sexual narcissists love approval, and they often use sex to get it. They will act so romantic and charming to gain your support.

8. They get mad when they're not sexually satisfied.

The self-esteem of most sexual narcissists' is based on getting approval of their sexual prowess. They will get angry and emotionally manipulate you to get what they want. They can also have an emotional outburst. Sometimes they will coerce you to give them what they want in the bedroom even if you do not like it. They will also threaten to tell everyone that it was your idea and try to brand you as a pervert.

If you have a narcissistic partner, the best thing for you is to drop that relationship. If leaving is difficult for you, you can see a therapist help you through the process.

Benefits of Great Sex

In a good, long-term relationship, there are several reasons why you and your partner should be having more sex. Higher frequencies of sexual activity have been associated with positive changes such as lower blood pressure, reduced stress, greater intimacy, and a lower divorce rate. There's no rule of thumb regarding sexual frequency, but there are some insights based on research.

A 2015 study discovered that overall well-being is linked with sexual frequency, but only to an extent. Relationship satisfaction greatly improved from not having sex at all to having sex once a week. It didn't go any higher at this point. Having sex once a week is pretty consistent with the current average. But our busy schedule can get in the way of our sex lives.

Standard Sexual Frequency

Regular adult: 54 times per year (about once per week).

Adults above 20: About 80 times annually

Adults in their 60s: 20 times annually

While frequency usually decreases with age, sexual activity in older adults is still vital. In general, older married couples have sex more often than their unmarried peers in the same age group.

Psychological Benefits of Sex

Sex has several emotional, mental, and psychological benefits. It has also been associated with longevity and a better quality of life. Some fantastic benefits of sex are:

1. **Improved self-image:** Sex can significantly increase your self-esteem and reduce feelings of insecurity. Improved self-image results in a more positive perception of ourselves.

2. Higher happiness levels: A recent 2015 study conducted in China showed more consensual sex and good quality sex increases happiness levels.

3. More intimacy: certain Brain chemicals are released when you have sex, including endorphins, which reduce irritability and feelings of depression. The hormone oxytocin increases when the nipple is being stimulated and when you engage in sexual activity. Oxytocin also gives you a sense of calmness and contentment.

4. Stress relief: Chronic stress can lead to few sexual encounters between married couples. But did you know that having sex is a great way to relieve stress? One round of great sex reduces your cortisol and adrenaline levels, and the effects last well into the next day.

5. Better quality of sleep: Orgasms activate the hormone prolactin release, which helps you sleep better.

*P*hysical Benefits of Having More Sex

1. Improved physical fitness: some women don't know that sex is good exercise. According to the American Heart Association, having sex is equivalent to engaging in regular physical activities, such as brisk walking and climbing two flights of stairs. The sex act tightens and tones your abdominal and pelvic muscles. An improved muscle tone leads to improved bladder control.

2. Enhanced brain function: Primary studies on rats discovered that more frequent intercourse was connected with healthier cognitive function and new brain cells. Similar results have since been found in human studies. A 2018 research conducted on more than 6,000 adults connected frequent sex with improved memory performance in adults above 50.

3. Better immune function: Having more sex has a positive effect on your immune function. Regular sex may even reduce your risks of catching a cold or the flu.

4. Decreased pain levels: The endorphins released during sex leads to so much more than a sense of well-being and calm. It has been proven that endorphins can reduce migraine and back pain.

5. Weight loss: a 30-minute roll in the hay burns an average of 200 calories. The brain chemicals released when you're having sex can reduce food cravings and support weight loss.

Beyond these individual benefits for you and your partner, having more boosts the health of your relationship. It increases intimacy and creates a stronger connection between you and your partner. In monogamous relationships, sex strengthens your commitment and stretches your bind.

How to Kickstart Your Sex Life

Sexual frequency changes over time. However, it doesn't mean that it should take a downward spiral. If you are wondering whether you can revive your sex life to be as good as it was when you fell in love, the answer is yes. Your sex life can improve; it just takes some extra work on your part. There are many ways to improve your sex life. And sometimes you have to look outside the bedroom.

It is often said that the biggest sex organ is the mind. Increasing sex frequency without focusing on the emotional connection or improving your communication is unlikely to give you lasting results. It would be best if you did not wait until your level of desire matches your partner's level, or else you will wait for a long time. Instead, talk to each other about your needs and find a compromise.

Sex Tips For Long Term Couples

If you have been married for a long time, the chances are that you are looking to spice up your sex life. However, you may feel like you have everything in the book. So here are some great tips that will help revive the fore in your sex life.

Engage in Power games.

Seduction is something that you and your partner can add to your sex life. Who is usually in charge of the bedroom? If you do not want to switch things up, who is the seducer, and who plays the seduced? Who dominates and who submits? It's good to explore these aspects of your love life. You can talk about these things with your partner and come up with ways to change things.

Seduce Your Partner

If you have stopped seducing your partner, you need to resume that. Seduction is a great way to add some sparks to your bedroom life. It is so easy for long-term couples to get so used to each other that you end up going through the motions. Instead of just hopping into bed and getting on top of each other, take things slow. Add some music, do a striptease and, let your partner's senses go wild.

Listen To Your Senses

Adding new things to your sex life can increase your mutual satisfaction. have you ever caught yourself worrying or thinking about something that has nothing to do with sex while under the sheets? Our minds tend to drift away during intimacy, and it is your job to bring it back to the present moment. Pay attention to your thoughts when you are having sex. It is called mindfulness, and it is the ability to be fully in tune with the present moment.

The Seduction Bowl

This is a fantastic game you can play with your partner. Get a bowl and write down all your fantasies and the naughty things you would like your partner would do to you. Then whatever your partner picks from the bowl is what he'll do to you. It goes both ways, and it will make your night extraordinary.

It's alright to Be Selfish.

Sex doesn't revolve around just you, but sometimes it's good to focus on your pleasure. For you to achieve complete arousal and satisfaction, you have to ask for what you want. Take note of what makes you tick and tell your partner. It would be best if you also did the same.

Be Kinky.

How many couples are afraid to express their deepest fantasies and get freaky with each other? Very few. But you are robbing yourselves of the joy of sex. Learn to tell each other everything and don't be afraid to get naughty.

Be Vulnerable with each other.

While being vulnerable is usually not the first thing on your mind, it's essential. If there is trust in your relationship. It would be best if you weren't afraid to show how much you enjoy your partner. It's alright to cry or moan to express your satisfaction. It makes the experience more intense and intimate.

Making Sex a Priority – Maintenance sex

A reduced sex drive can be expected in long-term relationships and marriages, but you must ensure that your sex life doesn't suffer. This is where 'maintenance sex' comes in. essentially, it's the concept of "not really in the mood but let's do it anyway.' It does not always have to be planned, but this has saved many marriages.

You and your partner have to sit down and talk about where you are at in your sex life and resolve to do something about it. It may be setting reminders or creating a schedule. Both of you may be into it at first. But the goal is to build intimacy and increase your sex drive.

However, not all sex should be maintenance sex. Discuss what works best for your relationship. Sex should prioritize both quality and quantity. Seek to fulfill your needs as best as you can. Here are some things you both can do to make things easier:

1. Keep your phones and any other gadget outside the bedroom.

2. Make sure that if you reach orgasm.

3. Find time to reconnect and get intimate outside the bedroom.

4. Eliminate stress.

5. Start your day with morning sex. It doesn't have to last for hours.

The Bucket List

Sex is not meant to be boring, but it can get stale when you keep on making the same moves over and over and over again. What makes sex interesting is change and variety. Here are some mind-blowing sex positions that you and your partner can try. Let's call it your bucket list.

Corkscrew

How to Do It: Sit near the edge of a bed and rest on

your hip and forearm. Gently press your thighs together. Your partner should straddle you while entering from behind. Having your legs pressed together will help you maintain a tight hold on your partner as he thrusts in and out of you. To make things hotter, thrust your hips as well.

Face-Off

How to Do It: Your partner should sit on a chair or the edge of the bed. Sit on his lap facing him. With this position, you control how deep his thrusts are. You also control the entry angle and is a great way to foster intimacy as you both stare into each other's eyes.

Doggy Style

How to do It: Go down on your knees while your partner kneels behind you. His upper body should be straight t or draped slightly over you while he enters you from behind. This position is excellent because it allows for stimulation of the G-spot and deep penetration. Your partner can also stimulate your clitoris.

Pretzel Dip

How to Do It: Lay down on your right side while your partner kneels, straddling your right leg. It would be best if you curled your left leg around his left side. This position also provides deep penetration and face-to-face contact. Your partner can also stimulate your clitoris while thrusting.

Flatiron

How to Do It: Lay face down on the bed and keep your legs straight as you raise your hips slightly. This position is excellent as it makes your partner's penis larger.

*S*ex is very important in marriage but does not allow the lure and excitement of great sex to keep you from noticing your partner's toxic traits. Sex is beautiful when the couple loves and respects each other.

CHAPTER 6
PLANNING YOUR EXIT STRATEGY

*I*f you are not happy in your relationship, you have to pay attention to what is causing it. If you are still wondering if you are in a healthy relationship or not, you can refer to chapter one, where I discussed how to identify a toxic man or toxic relationship. But here are some pointers. Your partner is toxic if he:

• Makes all the decisions in your life and the relationship.

• He always wants to know where you are at all times or constantly checks on you.

• Prevents you from seeing friends or talking to other people.

• Loves to Control what you were or who you spend time with

• It tells you to stop an activity that you love to do.

• Constantly insults and criticizes you.

- Loves to blame you or guilt-trip you about things you have not done in the relationship.
- Is physically, emotionally, and verbally abusive or threatens you with violence.
- Forces you into sex without your consent.
- Threatens to harm himself if you leave him.
- Makes excuses for his actions and attributes them to drugs or alcohol.

If he does all these things, then you are in a relationship with a toxic partner. There are some other indications such as:

- You cannot talk to them openly or cannot be yourself around them.
- You are never happy in the relationship.
- You always believe that you can fix other people.
- You are always worried about your safety and that of your loved ones.

If you are in a toxic relationship, it is a lot easier to leave. However, leaving an unhealthy marriage is much more complicated and trickier. In a relationship, you are only bound by love and commitment to each other. There are no legalities or religious bindings on you both. There are no strict societal expectations for you to meet. Marriage, on the other hand, is another ball game. That is why it is hard for married people, especially women, to leave their toxic husbands. When I got divorced, it was the most challenging part of my life. I was so afraid about what people would say. I thought about the effect it would have on my children. But I overcame my fears and did what I had to do to find happiness in my life.

Getting a divorce is not easy at all, and you have to be sure that you are doing it for the right reasons.

The Three Dilemmas

There are three dilemmas that women contemplating divorce usually face. Once you move beyond this stage, then you're ready to face the next phase of your life.

1. I want to get a divorce, but I don't know if it is the right thing to do.

Getting a divorce has a profound impact on your children's lives. It also affects your lifestyle, finances, and even your career. There is so much pressure to make the right decisions that you begin to rethink your decision. The truth is that there are no promises. The best thing to do is to go with your gut and not your emotions or ego.

2. My husband wants a divorce, not me.

If you are in this situation, you are probe to feel helpless and less in control. You will be devastated as you watch your life change without being able to do anything. You must ask yourself if you are hanging on to your marriage out of fear of the unknown. It is challenging to face your problems when your partner has so hurt you.

3. My marriage is not working; that is why I need a

divorce.

If this is where you are, then you are most likely to blame your partner for the breakdown of your marriage. You will be focused on the anger you feel for your partner because you believe that they have forced you to make an unpleasant decision. If you don't resolve the emotional turmoil in your mind, the divorce proceedings are bound to be messy and filled with tension.

The common problem in all these dilemmas is fear. If you don't deal with it and declutter your emotions, you will get a divorce, but it will be marked with tension and negative feelings, which will affect everyone involved, especially your children. For your children's sake, you must seek a peaceful divorce. It will also help you heal afterward. You may ask yourself: can I avoid all these conflicts and peacefully divorce my toxic husband? Yes, you can. I will discuss how to prepare for a divorce and the factors you should consider before getting a divorce. You must be prepared for it.

There are twelve factors you must consider before moving out of your matrimonial home. Every divorce is different, and everyone needs legal advice carefully suited to their individual's particular condition. All divorces are different, and every case necessitates legal advice tailored to the client's situation.

1. Financial implications.

Moving out is very important, but it can also be financially overwhelming. Set up a budget and seek the help of a financial planner.

2. Legal implications.

Moving out creates a myriad of legal complications that are expensive and difficult to deal with. Not to mention how emotionally and physically draining it is. You'll have to determine who will pay the mortgage, insurance, and taxes. You also have to decide whether you will be entitled to credits for underpayment or overpayment of the house.

3. Parenting.

Both of you have to reach a custody agreement. The court will also determine if you have the legal authority to take full custody of your children. Co-parenting is very important. You do not want your children to suffer from inconsistency and instability. As much as you can, shield your children from all the messiness that may come with the divorce.

4. Assets.

In some states like California, the law will require full disclosure of all assets, but some spouses try hard to hide vital information or assets. Compile all the documents of your assets, debts, and income on your PC. Prepare every document that will help you in your case. Personal properties can get lost in the shuffle, so make sure you take an inventory of your furniture and your belongings in your home.

Moving out is a big step, so do not make any hasty

financial decisions, such as signing a lease until you are sure you can afford it. Seek the services of a certified divorce lawyer. Deciding to divorce is only the first step. Your husband may want to fight the divorce, so there are a few things to do before you leave.

5. Ensure you have everything you need.

You must make sure that you can take care of yourself before you leave your marriage. If you have some money in a joint account, take some of it and transfer it to your account. Based on your state laws, this money is considered marital property, but doing this will make it more challenging for your spouse to gain access to your money.

If you do not have a job, you must make a suitable plan for your survival after the divorce. Don't assume your husband will pay your bills. Divorce usually brings out the monsters in some people. Some judges will ask the working spouse to cater to the other's needs during the divorce, but it's not guaranteed.

Be prepared to accept a living situation that is uncomfortable for a while. If you need to leave immediately, especially in physical abuse, seek shelter in your area. Moving to a homeless shelter may be uncomfortable, but you will be close to some resources in the area. You can also stay with friends and family until you can make it on your own. Just have a backup plan in place.

When you file for divorce, marital assets are placed on hold. It is beneficial as a working spouse is required to maintain health insurance for the nonworking spouse. However, there are some limits on the assets that can be sold and split. Learn your state laws before making any financial decisions.

6. Make Copies of Important Documents.

For paperwork, divorce is worse than paying for a home. It pays to have all the information you need. Making copies of all the critical documents in your home – tax returns, insurance paperwork, mortgage documents, etc. Keep them safe for when you will need them.

Additionally, do not assume that you can easily access any online accounts. Your spouse may change the password without telling you. Log in to all your joint accounts and take screenshots of all the vital information. Ensure you have account numbers and any other information you may need to recover.

7. Consult a good divorce attorney.

The safest way to locate an attorney that suits your needs is by word of mouth. You have to disclose your intents to at least one other person. If it is not proba-ble, go to online forums that display lawyers by geographic area and check for personal reviews.

Be specific and practical in what you want your attorney to do for you. They cannot offer you closure or emotional healing. No matter how the proceedings go. You will not be entirely pleased with the verdict. A judge can overrule your attorney, so don't be swayed by their promises.

Find an attorney that suits your needs. Ensure that you can afford their services and that they are experienced in cases like yours. You also have to be comfortable with them. You won't lose all you have after your divorce, and you may lose a lot of money. But think about the fact that you're walking away with your life, health, and dignity.

8. Strengthen Your Support Systems.

Divorce is not the time to be alone or try to do everything yourself. Talk to your family and friends and accept their support. You may want to wait till after the divorce is public before seeking support but decide beforehand who you can trust and lean on. You can seek the services of therapists or a coach to help you relieve stress. Avoid people who give you negative vibes. You may have to cut them loose.

Social Services can tell you about financial resources for single parents. Call the office closest to you. If they can't provide financial assistance or any kind of help you need, ask for other resources. Seek support from your church. Look for practical resources that can help you. You can also learn so much from women who have become financially independent and rebuilt their lives after leaving toxic marriages.

9. Decide How to Deliver the News.

This is usually the most difficult part. I will discuss this later in the book. However, do not be cruel or manipulative when telling your family. Remember that the goal is to become a better person and leave with grace and dignity.

· · ·

*H*elping Your children cope
Divorce is usually more complicated if you have kids. You have to think about explaining what is happening to your children, with or without your spouse. You also have to develop ways to help your children cope with the aftermath of the divorce.

10. Set Boundaries and create Structure in Your Schedule.

Divorce can leave a massive void in your life. You can be tempted to fill the void with harmful activities such as smoking and drinking. Additionally, we usually have better mental health when there are boundaries around us. The end of marriage breaks some of these boundaries, and you must replace them with healthy ones. Use this time to fill your schedule with healthy activities. I will show you how to recover after a divorce in the next chapter. There's help out there, but you must actively seek it.

11. Think strategically, not emotionally.

In his book A Woman's Guide To Financial Security After Divorce, Jeffrey Landers defines the essential first steps you must take after your divorce to achieve long-term financial stability and independence. You must learn how to support your goals and vision with a workable financial plan that guarantees your long-term financial security.

You cannot depend on your emotions when planning your future; you need to study reverse mortgages and why you should consider them. It's true that you need the money now but has to think about intelligent ways to use your investments and retirement accounts, and other sources of income to cover your financial needs. It would be best to learn which assets are most satisfactory and what strategies are best for managing liabilities. Acting will give you a sense of control in your life.

12. Take things one day at a time.

You can easily get overwhelmed, apprehensive, afraid, and discouraged about the journey you're about to embark on. Don't let pessimism or fear stop you from leaving a toxic husband! Stay focused on your dreams and how much better the divorce will be for you and your children. Write all the things you want to accomplish in a year. How much do you want to be making weekly or hourly? What kind of friends do you want to have a relationship with? How do you spend your time?

*G*et a journal, and write down all your hopes, dreams, and plans for the future. Do not allow your present circumstances to stop you from dreaming. Your thoughts have a huge part to play in creating your future. It is time to be the woman you're meant to be.

∼

CHAPTER 7
LEVEL UP

*N*ow you have gone through with the divorce, and your emotions are a mess. I felt the same way too. Different thoughts kept running through my head. I felt very lonely. But I had decided to take charge of my life. First of all, I will share some tips on sorting out your emotions and getting clarity.

Identify this for what it is: A pity party.

You can get so wound up in your emotions that you slip into a well of dramatic self-pity. I felt this way after my divorce, but I had to tell myself that it wasn't the 'abandoned' one. Tell yourself that you won't live any less because if you divorce. Tale all that emotional garbage out of your mind.

You are what you think! Your brain accepts anything I tell it.

You can choose the thoughts to dwell on. Opinions are like birds flying over our heads; you cannot prevent a bird from flying, but you stop it from perching on your head. When you begin to have those destructive thoughts, refuse to dwell on them. You can shift those thoughts from your mind and choose to focus on more positive ones.

Get a gratitude journal.

Apart from your regular journal, get another journal specifically for gratitude. Every day, write down three things that you're grateful for. It will boost your mental health and give you a positive outlook on life.

Laughter is still the best medicine.

When combined with music, it truly is the best medicine. I know it's difficult to find joy or reasons to laugh, but laughter heals the soul. Besides, if you take a look around you, you'll see that reasons to laugh.

Change is a part of life.

Believing otherwise will adversely affect your life and prevent you from healing. You may be feeling sad now, but as you take on new challenges and learn to find yourself again, things will change drastically in your life. It is a cycle. Learn to enjoy the different stages of your life and learn the lessons in them.

Go for a walk.

Physical exercise can result in mind-blowing changes. So go for a walk. Get a gym membership. Get into the shape of your dreams. Physical activity has so many great physical and mental benefits.

. . .

*W*rite down affirmations and paste them all over the house.

Write down affirming words and paste them all over your house. In the morning, recite them to yourself. Remind yourself of them throughout the day. Look in the mirror and say them to yourself. Repeat it before you sleep.

How to Manage the Lingering Loneliness After Divorce.

Overcoming the loneliness that comes after a divorce is hard. It is a lifelong process that you will have to deal with. As years go by, those harmful, painful emotions and memories will come back to you, but you must make a choice to deal with them or allow them to cripple you.

It's a choice you must make every day.

Getting through the hard times of divorce is difficult. It is a significant life event that will alter your emotions. Facing family members and attending family gatherings will trigger memories that you want to forget. Everyone will want to know what you are doing with your life after your divorce is over. It is a stressful period, but there are things you can do to soothe the lonely feelings you may have and get you through these challenging times.

. . .

*D*istinguish the Good things from the bad.

Take time each day to recognize the good things in your life. It could be your weekly nights out with friends, your Saturday shopping trips, a job or hobby that you enjoy, or volunteering at your hospital. Maybe it is time you have for yourself every Sunday night, watching your favorite movie or TV show, snuggling up with your cat while enjoying a delicious glass of red wine. These are the little things that you should write in your journal.

Focus on the Good things.

Let yourself be unhappy, angry, or upset when times are tough. But, once you have let yourself feel these emotions, get hold of yourself again. If you continue to do this, you won't stay sad or upset for long periods. It will help in your social life.

Spend enough time with your children. Know that your ex will always be a part of your life because of your kids. Don't dwell so much on it. Enjoy your time with your children.

Spread good wherever you go.

With all the help and knowledge you have learned, use it to help other women who are in a rough situation with their marriage. Our experiences aren't for us alone; they are meant for others as well. We use the lessons we learned to help other people. That is why I wrote this book.

. . .

*Y*ou can start afresh with your life and build something extraordinary out of it. Do things that make you happy and make others happy as well.

*T*he power of meditation

Meditation is extremely beneficial to your soul. While your body suffers from the endless anxiety of a divorce, you can get your mind quiet through meditation. When your mind is calm, it affects your body too, and you won't see outstanding results immediately but keep at it. Here are some things that you'll notice when you start.

Your stress levels will reduce drastically. Sometimes, it relieves so much that people stop taking anti-depressants and anxiety medications.

Meditation will energize you.

You will have less critical thoughts of yourself and others.

You will be happier.

You will be more patient with your divorce proceedings. The things your ex does won't bother you so much anymore.

You will make better decisions.

The quality of your sleep will increase.

You will have the ability to move on with your life, and your true self will start to emerge.

You will have a sense of purpose in your life.

You will develop the lifetime skill of training your mind to think positive thoughts.

*T*o gain all these benefits, you must do it. It takes discipline. You have to be committed to it. It will take time. You will be tempted to procrastinate but remind yourself about the benefits you will stand to gain. It will only take 25-30 mins. Try meditating twice a week and see how much better your mental health gets.

Get a chair and sit up straight on it. You can use a floor cushion or go for a slow walk on a safe path or sidewalk. Make sure you sit correctly and close your eyes. Breath slowly and listen to yourself as you breathe.

You will lose concentration at first, and that is okay. Realize that you are drifted and come back to the present.

Do it 25-30 minutes every morning. You can schedule another time if the mornings are not suitable for you. Just make sure you do it every day.

Keep this in mind: sometimes, when you're meditating, you might have feelings of intense fear, sadness, anger, or the opposite – joy, happiness, or contentment. Allow them to pass but keep on meditating. Go through the tears or laughter. The meditation will eventually help you get control of your emotions and declutter your mind.

· · ·

To get you started, recite the Prayer of St. Francis of Assisi. You can find any other peaceful prayer or affirmations that you like.

Make me an instrument of your peace.

Where there is hate, let me spread love.

In uncertainty, let me spread the faith.

In certainty, let me spread hope.

In the darkness, let me spread light.

In injury, let me spread pardon.

In sadness, let me spread happiness.

Let me not need to be consoled so much as to console.

To be loved, as to love.

To be understood, as to understand.

For, it's in the giving that we receive.

It's in the pardoning that we are pardoned.

It's in the letting go of our old ways that we are born to the new ways.

Remember that your mind believes anything you tell it, so begin to speak your mind that you want peace and happiness.

Some Coping Skills to Help You Make it Through.

No matter how peaceful your breakup is, divorce is still one of the most challenging and stressful experiences you will ever have. Like any significant life event, divorce upsets nearly all aspects of your life. From a practical perspective, you are shifting from living with a partner to living without one, which may affect your finances and maybe even change your housing situation. If you have kids, you will find yourself suddenly making co-parenting decisions with your ex-husband. It may look like that your whole world has turned upside down. Here are some self-care tips that will help you cope with the divorce:

Maximize Your Support System

As the Beatles famously said, "you can survive with a bit of help from your friends and family." Having a great support system of family members, good friends, and trusted co-workers is an excellent way to remind yourself that you're not alone. As much as you can, get as much face-to-face contact as possible with people who sincerely care about you, are ready to listen, and will offer sympathy and positive reassurance.

Everyone appreciates verbal partner-bashing after a breakup but doesn't stay in the past. Stay away from people who dwell on how awful your former partner treated you instead of helping you move on with your life.

Join a good Divorce Support Group

It is stated that one marriage ends every 13 seconds in the United States. This statistic shows that many people are going through the same difficult time as you are right now. That is why religious and community organizations have planned divorce support groups as a haven for people going through the divorce process to meet weekly or daily and talk about their feelings and experiences.

Long-time friends and family members will love you and give you support, but someone who has been through a divorce can provide a different kind of understanding. Relating the details of your partner's hurtful actions or sharing how much you cried while devouring a bowl of ice cream can be incredibly liberating, especially when others can genuinely sympathize and share the stories of their experiences with their exes.

Forge New Friendships.

A divorce will entail dividing finances, assets, time with children, and even friendships. Sometimes people who were friends with you and your partner as a couple may find it difficult staying close to you or being loyal to both of you. Some of your friends may leave you rather than stick by you to help you, and it's okay. Like I explained in a previous chapter, divorce may be an excellent opportunity to let go of some toxic friendships.

Allow yourself to form new relationships. It is a beautiful way to start fresh. Invite one of your child's parents for a cup of coffee or strike up a conversation with your colleague you haven't talked to before. It's an excellent way to form new and potentially long-lasting friendships.

Nurture New hobbies and Interests.

Depending on how your divorce goes, you may find that you have lots of time on your hands. Instead of using that time to dwell on your breakup, use it to learn something new. Bet a new hobby and develop the ones you already have. You can join a book club. Attend a seminar or take a course in continental cuisine. You will love the company as well as the distraction from your divorce-related problems.

Engage in Self-Reflection.

You are not to blame for your partner's toxic behavior, but there are some things that you may have done throughout your marriage that contributed to your divorce. Divorce tends to reveal many hidden things in a marriage. This is the time to do some self-reflection. Write your thoughts in your journal. The aim of self-reflection is not to trigger feelings of sadness or anger. You aim to reflect on yourself and how to make things better in your life. Applauds yourself for the good things you have done.

Take Proper Care of Yourself.

If you're not cautious, you can get entangled up in your divorce. You may experience insomnia or sink the depression. Self-care is very important. I have shared some self-care tips above, so ensure to practice those tips. Look good, treat yourself, and do not stop yourself from having fun. Do not neglect your needs. You can start with meditation and exercise. Self-care does not have to be elaborate but do not ignore it.

Don't spend time with a Long Legal Process.

When you and your spouse get divorced, find ways to make the divorce proceedings as quickly as possible. Divorces that take too long wreak havoc on your mental and emotional health. It will also affect your children. However, if your court proceedings will inevitably take a long time, spend time meditating. It's a much healthier way to deal with the stress of everything.

If you can, hire a divorce mediator to act as a go-between as you discuss your options. Many people say that the mediation experience fosters better communication between their partners during and after the divorce.

Ask for Professional Help

Your support network, divorce group, and new friends will help you recover from the breakup. But there are to your healthy recovery from your breakup in different ways. However, there are some issues that only a qualified mental health professional can solve—that why you must employ a therapist.

Individual therapy will help you heal properly after your divorce. A professional therapist will help you unearth the problems in your previous relationship, as well as your feelings and behavior. Your therapist will also help you make the transition from your life as a married woman to a new, single life. Lastly, if your mental health has been severely affected, a psychotherapist will help you recover.

The first time I grasped that my marriage was not going to end in divorce, I didn't want to tell my family or friends because I felt embarrassed and ashamed. But I didn't want to be someone who was constantly pitied because I got a divorce. So, I had to think of the best way to break the news to my friends and family.

Breaking the news to your family

Some couples tell their children about the situation together, but that may not happen in this situation. Families have a way of supporting their own, but it's still a very tricky thing to do. Here are some ideas on how to tell your family about your divorce.

Be Open And Honest

When you start going to court, rumors are bound to fly around. Your family will want to know the truth about what is happening. They will ask questions, and you must be ready to answer them. You can't run away from these questions forever.

When you're planning what to tell them, prepare your words. At first, whenever I saw an old friend who asked about my family, I would almost break down in tears built I had to find a way around it. I couldn't continue to evade their questions.

Think carefully about how you want to tell friends and family about your divorce. I made several mistakes at the time. I said many things that I shouldn't have. But I learned better and found a way to answer their questions correctly. Resist the urge to use cruel words in describing your partner. Please don't focus on how bad he was. Instead of saying, "he was a beast who tortured me throughout our marriage." Instead, say something like, "my husband made a few choices that affected our marriage, but I know something better waiting for me."

Prepare your response so that when you suddenly meet someone who doesn't know, you won't get caught unexpectedly.

Should I share every detail?

When talking to people about your divorce, you don't have to recount all the gory details of how they cheated on you or manipulated you. It's not necessary. You will feel tempted to share these details, but you shouldn't.

Telling Your Friends About the divorce

The way you tell your book club friends about the divorce is different from how you would tell your church members you have known for 20 years. It's also different from how you tell the parents of your kids' friends.

It's usually hardest to tell your new friends, neighbors, and acquaintances about the divorce. Just be careful only to state the facts and keep it simple. They don't have to know all the details.

What happens when you lose your Friends Because Of Divorce?

Divorce can be hard on friendships. They do not know the entire story. They may have different stories from both of you. They may also get torn between both of you, especially if they have any connection with your ex. Most people will remain neutral, but eventually, things will get complicated.

Usually, it's the women who lose the most friends. Reconnect with your old friends and maintain your friendship and with some of your couple friends' wives. Creating new relationships can also help.

Telling your Co-Workers

You may not believe this, but colleagues and co-workers can be excellent sources of support during a divorce. They will easily support you because they have no relationships with your ex. Talk about your divorce with your boss and colleagues. But make sure that they're the kind of people you can trust.

What Will 'They' Say?'

Prepare yourself for different responses when you are telling people about your divorce. The answer you get is a direct result of the story you tell them, so be wise. If you express anger, chances are they will be angry as well. If you display grace and dignity, they will respond in that way too.

Unsolicited Advice

Most times, when you tell someone about your divorce, they may not comprehend how you feel, especially if they've never had such an experience. Some people will be helpful, but others will say inappropriate things such as:

You're much better without him!

Get over him! He's not worth it!

Move to another state; it will help.

You need to get a new guy, so you don't get lonely.

Religious Objections

This may be an excellent time to think deeply about your religious beliefs. Having something higher than life to believe in is very important and will help you heal.

Some spiritual groups have solid and strict concepts about marriage and divorce. Some believe that it's wrong to get a divorce for any reason except infidelity. There are other ways to be unfaithful in your marriage. Any form of abuse (physical, emotional, financial, substance abuse) is a betrayal of your promises to love, honor, and cherish your spouse.

Are you sharing the news on Social Media?

I do not think it's necessary to share the news about your divorce on your social media platforms. Certain things in life shouldn't be announced on social media. Most times, it will only make things worse. But if you feel you have to, follow the tips above. Display grace and dignity instead of anger and rage.

CHAPTER 8

HELPING CHILDREN COPE WITH THE
DIVORCE

*D*ivorce has the worst effect on children, and
every year, thousands of children experience the traumatic stress of divorce. Their reaction
usually depends on their personality, age, and the
nature of the separation and the divorce proceedings.

∼

*C*hildren are always negatively affected by
divorce, and the typical reaction is sadness,
anger, shock, frustration, resentment, or worry. But
children can learn how to cope with the aftermath of a
divorce and go on to become more flexible and well-
balanced adults. There are some vital things that you
can do to help your children heal and cope with the
stress of the divorce:

- Keep your children away from conflict,

heated discussions, and all kinds of talk about divorce.

- Limit the interruptions to their daily routines.
- Let every negativity and blame be limited to private therapy sessions or conversations with friends outside the home. Do not bring such discussions into your home.
- Do not keep your ex away from your children unless he's violent or poses a considerable threat to their well-being.
- You must seek support from your friends, professionals, clergy, and family during this difficult time. But never use your children as a support system, even if it looks like they want you to.

~

*H*ow to reveal the news to your children
When you have made up your mind, tell your children about your decision to live apart from your spouse. While there is no easy or painless way to break the news, if possible, you and your ex should talk to your children about it. Resist the urge to express feelings of anger, guilt, or blame during the conversation. You can practice how you are going to manage the conversation to avoid getting upset when the time comes.

You should talk to them according to their age,

temperament, and level of maturity. However, your conversation should always emphasize that what happened between you and your ex has absolutely nothing to do with them. Many children feel guilty because they believe their parents divorced because of them even after you have tried to convince them otherwise. You have to keep reassuring them.

Let your children sometimes know adults change how they love each other or disagree on certain things, so they have to live separately. But tell them that they will always be a part of their parents' lives forever. Parents and their children don't agree on everything, but that's only a part of life. Parents and children never stop loving each other and or get separated from each other.

Give them enough information so that they can prepare for the changes in their lives. Answer their questions as best as possible, and don't try to lie or cover up anything. Try to answer their inquiries as truthfully as possible. Keep in mind that kids don't need to know all the reasons behind a divorce (especially if it has something to do with the other parent). You don't have to start telling your children how toxic your partner is. They only need to be explained what will change in their daily routine and will not.

For younger children, it's best to keep it simple. You can say: "mom and dad are going to live in separate houses, so they don't fight so much, but we both love you very much."

. . .

*O*lder children and teenagers may better understand what their parents have been going through and might have more questions based on what they have heard and noticed from conflicts and fights.

~

*H*ow to handle your children' reactions

Expect your children to be upset. Tell them that you acknowledge and understand how they feel. They have a right to feel that way, so do not try to invalidate their feelings. You can say something like: "I know you are very upset about this, and I completely understand. We love you so much, and we are sorry that we have to live separately. Can we try to think of something that would make you feel better?"

Some children do not react immediately. Don't try to get a reaction out of your children. Let them respond in their way. Let them comprehend that you are always there for them whenever they're ready. Some children will act as though everything is okay to please their parents. They may deny any hurt feelings they have. Sometimes, these hidden feelings could be expressed in other ways. Their grades may begin to drop, and they will act out in the presence of their friends, changes in behavior and sleeping patterns, etc. No matter how your children react to your divorce, they will want to know how it will affect their own lives. <u>Prepare yourself for questions like:</u>

Will I live with you or dad?

Do I have to go to another school?

Do I have to move?

Where will both of you live?

Where will we spend our holidays?

Will I still get to visit my friends?

Can I still go camping this summer?

Can I still do my favorite activities?

It is not easy to be honest, especially when you don't have all the answers to these questions. You might feel helpless, especially when they are feeling scared or guilty about what's happening. The right thing to do is to tell them what they need to know at that point.

Helping your children cope with the stress.

Many children and parents mourn the loss of the ideal family they had hoped for. Children miss having both parents around and the good times they shared. That's why most children continue to hope that their parents will someday come back together — even after the finality of divorce has been explained to them over and over again.

. . .

*I*t is normal to grieve the loss of a family. However, with time, both you and your children will come to accept the new circumstances. Let them know that it's alright to wish that their parents will get back together and explain the certainty of your decisions.

~

*H*ere are some tips to help your children cope with the stress of divorce:

• Promote honesty. Children should know that their feelings are valid and vital to their parents and that they'll be taken seriously.

• Help them express their feelings with words. Children's behavior can give you an insight into their emotions. You can say: "it seems as you are feeling sad right now. Do you know why you feel so sad?" be a good listener, even if it will hurt to hear what they have to say.

• Accept and validate their feelings. Telling them that you understand and acknowledge their feelings will show your children that their feelings are valid. It is essential to encourage children to get it all out before you start talking about making it better. Let your children grasp that it is alright to feel happy, relieved, or excited about the future.

• Give them support. Ask the children what will

make them feel great. They might not be able to pinpoint anything, but you can offer some ideas — maybe to sit together, go for a walk, or hold their favorite teddy bear. Younger children may appreciate it if you call their daddy on the phone.

• Stay healthy. Separation and divorce are highly stressful. The pressure can be worsened by custody battles, property, and financial issues, usually bringing out the worst in people. Finding ways to deal with stress is essential for you and your family. Keep yourself as physically and emotionally healthy as possible to help you manage the effects of stress. When you take care of your needs, you will be in the best shape to help your children as well.

• Be discreet about the details you share. Ensure privacy when speaking about the details of the divorce with friends, family, or your lawyer. As much as you can, let your conversations with your ex be as polite and civil as possible, especially when you're interacting in the presence of your children.

• Resist the urge to blame or insult your ex in front of your children no matter the circumstances of your divorce. This is especially vital when the divorce is a result of something as hurtful as infidelity. Keep all letters, emails, and text messages secure as children will be naturally curious if there is conflict at home.

• Seek help. Now is not the time to try and do everything on your own. Look for a good support group, talk to other people who have gone through a divorce, make use of online resources, or ask your doctor or religious leaders to refer you to credible resources. Seeking help for yourself is an excellent example for your children and will teach them the right way to deal with significant life changes. Seeking help from a therapist or friend will also help maintain boundaries with your children. It is essential not to look to your children for support. Older children may try to make you feel better by giving you a shoulder. Despite how tempting that is, they should not be your source of emotional support. Let your children know how much you value their care and kindness, but do not vent your feelings to them. Do that with your friend or counselor.

~

The importance of consistency

Consistency and routine can provide comfort that can help your family during this important transition. If possible, reduce unpredictable schedules, changes, or abrupt separations.

Amid a divorce, children will benefit greatly from spending time with each parent. Despite how inconvenient it is, allow your ex to visit your children.

Naturally, you'll be worried about how your child is dealing with this change. The best you can do is trust your instincts and lean on what you know about your children. Are they acting differently than usual? Is your child regressing to younger behaviors, such as thumb-sucking or bedwetting? Are their emotions interfering with their everyday routines, like school and social life?

You must look out for behavioral changes such as mood swings, sadness; anxiety; school issues; or difficulties with relationships, changes in appetite, and sleep can be signs of a problem.

Older children and teenagers may be susceptible to risky behaviors such as alcohol and drug use, skipping classes, and defiant activities. Notwithstanding whether such troubles are associated with the divorce, they are serious issues that affect a teenager's well-being and indicate professional help.

Fights and quarrels in front of the children

While it's expected to have occasional arguments between parents in any family, living in a state of continual hostility and unresolved conflict can burden a child. Constant screaming, fighting, arguing, or violent acts can frighten children and make them worried.

Parents who engage in conflicts in front of children set a terrible example for their children learning how to develop relationships. When children are in an environment of constant war, they're more likely to have emotional and behavioral problems that continue into adulthood.

Seeking help from a divorce counselor or counselor can help couples share their grievances and hurt each other in a way that negatively affects their children. While it won't be easy to work together, it will protect your children from continued anger, sadness, and bitterness.

~

*a*dapting to a new living situation
Since divorce is a huge change, adjustments in living arrangements should be dealt with gradually. You can consider different kinds of living situations such as:

• One parent has sole custody of the children.

• Joint custody where legal and physical custody is shared.

• Joint custody where one parent has "tie-breaking" authority in some medical or educational situations.

• Which living situation will work best for your children? It's a difficult question and the one that couples have the most disagreement about. While some children won't mind spending half their time with each parent, others need the stability of having one parent at home and visit with the other parent. Some parents decide to live in the same house — but this only works in scarce circumstances and is not advised.

. . .

*W*hatever arrangement you decide, put your child's needs first. Don't get in a tug of war or a battle to win. When deciding how to celebrate holidays, birthdays, and vacations, focused on what's best for the children. Parents need to decide on these matters themselves. Never ask your children to choose.

In their preteen years, when children get more involved with activities without their parents, they may require different schedules to make room for their changing priorities. Children benefit best when there is continued support from both parents; however, they may resist equal time-sharing if it disrupts their academic or social lives. Listen to what they think about time-sharing and try to adjust.

Your child may resist sharing time with you and your ex equally and may choose sides. If this happens, as tricky as it is, don't take it personally. Keep the visitation schedule and focus on your importance and your partner being active in your children's lives.

Children may suggest spending a whole summer, semester, or school year with your ex if you have full custody. But don't decipher it as a desire to move in with your ex. Listen to them and consider these options if they're suggested. This arrangement can work well in peaceful divorces, but it is not common in higher-conflict situations.

~

*P*arenting under pressure

As much as you can, both of you should maintain schedules and discipline the same in both households. When there are similarities in bedtime schedules, rules, and homework, it will eliminate anxiety, especially in younger children.

Although you cannot implement the rules in your ex's home, maintain them in yours. Becoming lenient, especially in this period of change, tends to make children insecure and less likely to acknowledge and respect parental authority. Buying gifts as a substitute for love or allowing children to act out will not benefit them in the long run. Instead, show them affection. You cannot over-pamper your children with hugs or encouraging words.

Divorce is a big crisis for a family. But, if you and your ex can work together for the sake of your children, your family unit will continue to be a source of strength, even if stepparents get involved later. Here are a few things to keep in mind:

• Seek help to deal with your own painful emotions concerning the divorce. If you can adjust, your children will be more likely to do so.

• Take things easy. Take your time and allow your child to do the same. Emotional problems, loss, and hurt after divorce typically take time to heal, and it happens in phases.

• Pay attention to the signs of stress. Talk to your

children's teachers, doctor, or a child therapist for advice on dealing with specific problems that worry you.

Change, of any kind, is always tricky. Keep in mind that you and your children can and will go through this change. Look into yourself and find inner strength. Seek help and learn coping skills. It will be difficult, but it will make a big difference in helping your family survive this difficult time.

Becoming a single mom

Believe me when I say that I know exactly how you feel because I have been where you are. The year you become a single mom after a divorce is one of the most extended years of your life. You must prepare yourself for a year of many emotional highs and lows, self-doubt, and making many mistakes. But if you are the kind of single mom that is determined to make this year a good one for you and your children – despite the significant change – then this year can also be a good one.

*Y*ou may be thinking that divorce will bring doom for you and your children. But you can choose to change things.

You must decide to be the mom who refuses to watch helplessly as her family defends into a pool of misery. Divorce doesn't have to produce messed-up children, a life of ruin, or constant battles with your ex.

Based on both my research and my personal experience, you and your children can not only survive but thrive after this divorce. Do you want to know how to accomplish this? It does not necessarily have to do with your income, your ex, or your educational qualifications. It doesn't matter whether you have custody of your children or not. It doesn't even depend on the age of your children.

The secret to surviving divorce is maintaining a positive mindset, a loving relationship with your children, and tons of hard work.

~

*H*ere is a list of 6 common challenges you'll face in your first year as a single mom. Also, I included some solutions to help you deal with each of these challenges. If you want to make the most of this period and do what is best for your children, try your best to adhere to my advice.

1. Your self-esteem will temporarily reduce.

The Challenge: In the first year of single parenting, prepare to doubt every decision you make.

You can agree with this, right? After consulting with your partner about everything from childcare decisions to financial issues, you get to the point where you have to make every decision on your own with nothing but your instincts, values, and beliefs guiding you.

You might also feel unloved, vulnerable, and lonely. Divorces can wreck our sense of self-worth.

Even though it is normal to feel this way in the early stages of a divorce, it shouldn't define who you are.

How to handle it: in this first year of being a single parent, look for your inner courage and push yourself to try new things and explore new passions. Yes, you might find that you hate painting, for instance, but you will have learned some valuable things about your unique self. Tap into the woman you were before you got married and explore the hobbies you haven't thought about for years or the ones you have always wanted to try.

Also, you must not try to solve complex problems with shallow solutions. Do not go from one bad post-divorce relation to another one to avoid feeling lonely. You might start to doubt your beauty, and this will continue after your divorce and show in your new relationship unless you work on yourself.

Work at rediscovering the fantastic person you are so that when the time comes, you'll attract the right partner.

2. Many people will judge you.

The Challenge: let's face it, people can be cruel. They love to judge other people for different reasons but mostly because it makes them feel good about themselves. Such people think like, "well, my life is a mess, but at least it's not as bad as theirs." such thoughts make them comfortable.

How to handle it: you cannot change such people, but you can surround yourself with supportive and positive people. When people critically talk about your divorce, refuse to dwell on their comments. Such statements speak more about the person's character than you. As much as you can, please continue with your day and don't think about what they said.

3. You will have a fair share of mistakes and successes.

The Challenge: being a single parent is new to you, and it will involve a huger learning curve. The surest way to avoid making any mistakes is not to make any decisions at all! There's nothing worse than sitting back and refusing to live because you are afraid of making the wrong decisions.

On the contrary, you will make some amazing decisions that will positively impact your family life. The happiness you feel when this happens is terrific because as you try new things and observe that you're making the right decisions, your self-confidence and self-esteem will increase.

How to handle it: Cut yourself some slack – don't expect to get it right all the time. The best way to accumulate a portfolio of successful decisions is by making some bad decisions. You can set yourself up for success by maintaining a support group of trusted family and friends who can seek advice concerning new choices.

4. Your ex will get on your nerves.

The Challenge: you would not have gotten a divorce if you were head over heels for your ex. The first year of single parenthood means that both you and your ex are trying to work out this new situation. It means your ex will do things that will make you want to tear his hair out and scream, and this is entirely normal.

How to handle it: With tons of compromise, patience, and hard work, the chances are that you and your ex can find a method to work things out concerning parenting without tearing each other apart. It won't be easy, and you must be determined to be accommodating and perseverant if you want peaceful co-parenting. Your children will be grateful to you for doing your best to accommodate your ex. Compromise only applies if you had a somewhat amicable divorce. If your ex was abusive, has a mental illness, is an addict, you have to be strong enough to endure tedious custody hearings and decide not to get embroiled in unnecessary drama your ex will create. If he chooses not to be involved in your children's lives, be prepared to be mom and dad to them.

5. Accept the fact that your ex will have different rules at their house.

The Challenge: You're not the only one with a new life as a single parent; your ex is also trying to navigate this change so prepare yourself for different rules. Maybe, your ex let them watch tv till 11 pm while lights out at your home is at 9 pm.

How to handle it: The difference in household rules is quite common with divorced families, and (believe it or not) children are capable of adjusting to these different rules. Of course, children will prefer the more lenient rules – they may also complain to you if your rules seem to be stricter than your ex's rules. That's perfectly fine.

You are in charge of your household; as long as your practices are reasonable based on your values and beliefs, your children will learn to adjust to this.

6. Your children will misbehave.

The Challenge: whenever your child misbehaves, you will tend to blame yourself or your ex. But that's not necessary. All children misbehave. It is all part of childhood.

All children from traditional families, single families, and divorced families act out at one time or another. No child is perfect, and sometimes children learn from their mistakes.

Do you remember that line from the batman movie? Where Bruce Wayne's dad asks him why we fall? Bruce tells him that it's so we can learn how to get up again. You can apply this lesson to your children. Sometimes, they need to fail to succeed. As adults, we can also learn from our mistakes.

How to handle it: Plan for when your children misbehave. It should include:

A warm explanation

Clear expectations for behavior

Clear communication of consequences

Consistency

The best thing that you can do for your children in this first year of single parenthood is to show them that you love them and care for them even when they misbehave or get confused. Your love should be constant and unwavering.

You got this!

~

Following these tips will prepare you to be a great single mom. We all have our unique problems and challenges. We have to learn how to be flexible and creative to handle them.

Starting your first year as a single mom

Practice purposeful parenting – if you have a positive attitude about your divorce, your children will be more confident about conquering the first year even if you don't feel like it.

Take care of yourself - don't feel guilty about taking time for yourself. Go out with your friends, go to the spa, get a manicure, take a warm bath. It doesn't just prepare you mentally and physically to take on new challenges. It is also an excellent example for your children and shows them that taking care of yourself in difficult times is a good thing.

If you must, let go of critical, negative family and friends and surround yourself with positive influences.

Take care of your children's needs as soon as possible. If you're not careful, minor problems will get out of control. If your children need some support with adjusting to the divorce, get them the help they need. There is nothing wrong with getting therapy, tutors, or showing them extra attention during this difficult period. Don't get so caught up in your word that you ignore the cries of help from your child.

Be in charge of your household – do not give your children authority because you are having guilty feelings about the divorce. Your children need you to lead them even if it looks like they doubt your incompetence. Children are great at putting up a tough front, but the only thing they want is for you to put your arms around them and tell them that everything will be alright.

Acknowledge that you are doing your best. You can do this. Give yourself some credit. You deserve it.

Don't treat your children as your friends, your therapist, or your partner. Allow them to be children.

Set realistic expectations for the divorce, for your children, and yourself. Do not expect to figure out everything too soon. If you set the bar too high, you will be frustrated and disappointed for not meeting them. You are not perfect, and there is absolutely nothing wrong with that.

Like I said earlier, my children and I went through this, and we survived. I know you doubt if you can pull this off, but I am telling you that you can. If I did it, you could do it too.

∾

*G*etting out of bed in the aftermath of a divorce is definitely a huge challenge, let alone planning your future spent on your own. Still, along the line, you will begin to see that you are so much more than your relationship status and that life can get better after divorce.

Here are 12 amazing things that you'll discover about your life after a divorce:

1. Your free time is entirely yours to do as you wish.

2. You will never think of divorce to be a confidence booster, yet you'll discover that it can be.

3. If you get full custody of the kids, you determine how you will raise them.

4. You will find that you don't have to walk on eggshells anymore. You can face life with boldness.

5. If you have toxic in-laws, you no longer have to deal with them anymore.

6. If you are an every-other-weekend parent, you will enjoy some excellent benefits that come with it.

7. You will realize that your partner was not good for you.

8. You now have the opportunity to become a much better parent.

9. You no longer have to keep your ideas and dreams on the back burner.

10. You can sleep peacefully without fear or anxiety.

11. You will find yourself again and regain your self-worth.

12. There is LIFE after your divorce.

$\sim$

*H*ere are six extraordinary ways to kick-start your new life after divorce:

1. Make Yourself a Priority

After spending time with someone who didn't care about your needs, you can change things now and make yourself the center of your world. Please don't focus on how they will do after the divorce. Focus on taking care of yourself. Do those activities you used to relish before you got married. It may be as little as going back to college or taking that course you always wanted,

Also, pampering yourself should be a regular thing. Go to the spa or take long drives in the open air. Go to your best restaurant or the movies. Start living your life without limits. Put yourself first for once.

2. Let it Go, period.

"If you don't let go, if you don't forgive yourself, if you don't forgive what happened, if you refuse to realize that it's all over, you won't move on." Steve Maraboli made this statement, and it is imperative. These are the things you shouldn't do after your divorce. If you keep hanging on to them, you won't make progress in your life. Do not keep going over why your marriage didn't work. Face the reality that it's over, and you have so much to do and give.

Holding on will cause you pain and delay your healing process. Remind yourself that your marriage ended for a reason. Allow yourself time to heal completely. If you find that you occasionally remember the good memories you had with your ex, don't beat yourself up over it like it is normal. However, if you find it difficult to let go, seek help from a therapist.

Counseling and therapy will help you navigate through your feelings and help you let go of the past. That's what your divorce is now: your past.

3. Reunite with Old Friends

After divorce, you may lose the familiar friends you shared with your spouse. It is normal, so do not feel sad about it. Do not spend so much time worrying about it. Instead, reconnect with your old friends. It may be challenging, but it starts with a phone call or text message. Creating a social circle will help you heal properly.

4. Study how to Handle Your Finances

Understanding economics and investments may not have been necessary for you when you were married, but it is your responsibility now, mainly because you have kids to take care of. So, learn and become an expert in managing your finances. List all your income, expenditure, expenses, including assets and liabilities. It will help you check on your incoming versus the outgoing flow of money. It is also a reasonable basis for planning your monthly budget.

Although, if you don't have a job, consider building a career and learning new skills. It will boost your self-confidence and keep you busy. Making these small changes and staying mindful of how much you spend will help you monitor your finances.

5. Go on a mini-vacation and Travel.

Getting used to the single life is pretty tough. You may need to get away from everything and take a few days or weeks off. Go somewhere that you have always wanted to go to. It does not have to be expensive.

Plan a trip with some close friends or check for single people's tour groups and go on an exciting adventure. Taking a trip by yourself or alone with your children might seem outrageous, but it is an excellent way to get some perspective about your life and help you realize that you are stronger than you thought. Always remember that you survived a toxic marriage and gained your freedom.

6. Don't say goodbye to romance.

If you have recently been over a divorce, dating

again is not advisable. It would be best if you had time to heal and recover. However, it does not mean you should give up on love. There are many good men out there who will make you very happy. But start dating again only when you have recovered mentally and have fully healed internally from your divorce. If you do not give yourself the time to do your inner shadow work, you will carry a lot of emotional junk into your new relationship. **Shadow Work is** how you combine the aspects of your unconscious mind into your conscious reality and allow the positive characteristics of the **shadow** to express themselves. When properly used and channeled, the **shadow-self** has qualities that you can use to further your personal growth.

*K*eep these two important things about dating after divorce:

1. Do not compare other men to your ex.

2. Be careful and do not invest so much time and energy into someone until you have known them better.

If you thought living your new life after divorce would be difficult, follow these tips above and watch how your life transforms. Remember that it's all about you, so don't be afraid to break the rules. If love comes around, do not deny it but welcome it onto your life.

. . .

What You shouldn't do After a Divorce

You deserve to feel hurt and angry, but you don't have to allow those feelings to take over your life. You will survive this and come out a better person. Here are some essential things you should not do after a divorce.

1. Do not say or do anything to your ex out of malice.

Your emotions are probably still raw, but that's it's not enough reason to let your anger determine your actions. Resist the urge to throw out the snarky comments in your head, and if you're planning to do anything that will not benefit you in any way but will only remind your partner about how bitter you are, pause for a moment. Allow time to pass and get a grip on your emotions. Don't be in a hurry to make decisions.

2. Do not ever make your kids take sides.

Nothing makes a divorce more painful and damaging than dragging your kids into it. You must be honest with them about the divorce, but do not drag them into the mess that comes with it. Never make them take sides. It will damage their mental health. They love you both, so don't change it.

3. Do not jump feet first into the dating scene.

Even if you are emotionally ready to start dating, don't rush anything. Take time to know the person. You're not in a competition with your spouse to see who moves on faster. Dating again is not the solution to your problems. Give yourself time to be single. You will find it very enjoyable.

4. Do not spend money recklessly.

Don't be misled into thinking that buying Hermes bags or designer clothes will take away the post-divorce stress and complications. I have already shown you the best ways to deal with the stress of a divorce. You have to face your feelings so don't add more problems to your current situation. There are healthier ways to feel good about yourself, so don't plunge yourself into debt because of your divorce.

5. Do not dwell so long in sadness.

You will be sad and hurt, which is perfectly normal and expected. But don't get sucked into those negative feelings. Remember that you will always have a choice to make; you can choose to dwell in sadness and pain or use those feelings as a motivation to put yourself out there and achieve your dreams.

6. Do not share too many details about your divorce on social media.

Oversharing online would be vital, especially if you had a messy divorce. Don't give in to the urge to air all your dirty laundry online. Perhaps you want to blow off some steam and get some sympathy, but it will only make you a better person. Refrain from talking about your divorce on social media. Only your family and close friends can know about it.

7. Do not think that you will never see your ex again.

I know that you may long for a clean break, but it will not come so easily. If you have kids together, they will always be a part of your life. Learn to accept that you cannot cut them out of your life and if you run into them, resist the urge to be violent. Remember our motto, ladies: grace and dignity. Be civil and polite to them. It is a sign of maturity, and in turn, you will even gain their respect.

A NEW BEGINNING

It's been a pretty rough journey. However, at least you can throw away your fears because you are provided with enough information about how to deal with a toxic husband, how to identify toxic traits, and how to cope after a divorce. You are strong, and you can survive a toxic marriage and go through a divorce. You will also do so with grace and dignity. Remember all the tips discussed in this book and stick to them.

Divorce can be frightening, but it's a lot better than staying in a toxic marriage that will destroy your sense of self. Breaking free gives you back your self-worth and helps you to achieve your dreams. If you are still afraid, find strength from my story. I would never have written this book or fulfilled my dreams if I had caved in out of fear and stayed in my marriage. You don't have to be afraid. There are tons of women who have made something beautiful out of their lives after a divorce.

~

*P*lease take note of the toxic traits and watch out for them. Use the tips in chapters one – three to deal with the mind games and tricks that toxic men use. If sex is the major problem in your marriage, practice the tips I shared in chapter four. They will help to rekindle the sparks in your marriage. If you are about to get a divorce and frightened about the consequences, I have shared all you need to know about getting a divorce. You are armed with loads of information to help you make the right decisions in your life. Finally, you remember that you are strong and capable of doing whatever you want to do. Do not be afraid to take back your life and achieve your dreams. I will be cheering you on along the way! So go out there and be the beautiful, graceful, and dignified woman that you are meant to be.

CONCLUSION

The problem with toxic husbands is you do not always see their narcissism before marriage. Eventually, you will have to stop believing his promises and begging. You have to recognize that this is a toxic marriage and is not love at all. Because over time, you will end up losing yourself. There is no changing him. Honestly, you are sacrificing your life, and time is not infinite. Many of us are in denial about being in a toxic relationship. Once we realize they are toxic and the relationship is unhealthy, it is hard to leave them, hard to let go. It will take courage to move, money, and a combined effort of a therapist to start a new life.

Once you decide to regain control of your life and leave him, the best way to begin the process is to set time aside to develop a plan for you and any children involved with the separation. Such as putting money aside, praying, meditating, and having open communication with people who genuinely are there for you. This is not an easy process, but remember that your children are better when they see that you are healthier and happier.

Humbly and readily accept that you will feel some hurt and some pain until you get over and out of this relationship. You will encounter feelings of loneliness, uncertainty, grief, and loss until you move through the healing process and restore yourself and your life!

JUST FOR YOU!

Remember to go to: chelsealoxley.com for your free copy of my personal overnight guide: Fix Your Crown, a Femininity Manifesto and begin your level up journey now!

Special just for You!

FREE GIFT TO OUR READERS

ACKNOWLEDGEMENTS

First and foremost, I would like to thank: God for giving me the strength and courage to do this book. My friends and family have supported me throughout my journey to becoming a writer. A special thanks to every person that purchased a copy of my book. And to the individuals who wrote such great lessons that inspired me to share and to help others:

Patrick Wanis Ph.D. (DEC 21, 2017). 14 Steps to Get Out Now Of Toxic Relationship or Marriage. https://www.patrickwanis.com/14-steps-to-get-out-now-of-toxic-relationship-or-marriage/

Darlene Lancer, JD, LMFT, (Posted April 3, 2019). How to Leave a Narcissist or Toxic Relationship. https://www.psychologytoday.com/us/blog/toxic-relationships/201904/how-leave-narcissist-or-toxic-relationship. Darlene Lancer 2019.

Lisa A. Romano, (Mar 22, 2019). Letting Go. https://www.lisaaromano.com/blog/self-care-letting-go

Sofo Archon, The Unbounded Spirit, True Love vs. Toxic Love: 14 Core Differences https://theunboundedspirit.com/true-love-vs-toxic-love-14-core-differences/

Exploring your mind, (03 May, 2021) Toxic love relationships. https://exploringyourmind.com/toxic-love-relationships/

Allan Schwartz, LCSW, PH.D. (2020 mentalhealth.net) Narcissistic vs. Antisocial or Sociopathic Personality Disorders. https://www.mentalhelp.net/blogs/narcissistic-vs-antisocial-or-sociopathic-personality-disorders/

Cosmopolitan, (APR 23, 2019). How these women realized they were the toxic partner in their relationship. https://www.cosmopolitan.com/uk/love-sex/relationships/a27237447/women-toxic-relationship/

Samantha Darby, (Dec. 9, 2015) 13 Signs You Have A Toxic Spouse Who's Poisoning You & Your World. https://www.romper.com/life/13-signs-you-have-a-toxic-spouse-whos-poisoning-you-your-world-1990

Jon Johnson, on (June 21, 2020), Medically reviewed by Timothy J. Legg, Ph.D., CRNP. What to know about toxic masculinity. https://www.medicalnewstoday.com/articles/toxic-masculinity

Amanda Mull, (January 10, 2019), Psychology Has a New Approach to Building Healthier Men. https://www.theatlantic.com/health/archive/2019/01/traditional-masculinity-american-psychological-association/580006/

Lucio Buffalmano, (September 19, 2019), 10 Games

Men Play, And How to Handle Them. https://thepowermoves.com/games-men-play/. Power University.

Bustle Editors, (Updated: Oct. 8, 2019), 13 Things All Long-Term Couples Should Try In Bed. https://www.bustle.com/wellness/125942-13-things-all-long-term-couples-should-do-in-bed

Marissa Gainsburg and Nicole Blades, (JUL 30, 2020), This Is What Your Sex-Position Bucket List Should Look Like. https://www.womenshealthmag.com/sex-and-love/a19943165/sex-positions-guide/

Susie Brown, (September 2020), How To Leave Your Husband. https://www.midlifedivorcerecovery.com/how-to-leave-your-husband/

ABOUT THE AUTHOR

Chelsea Loxley is an Emerging Author & Breakthrough Life Coach.

Social media details:
  facebook.com/AuthorChelsea
  instagram.com/chelseatalksrelationships
  twitter.com/ChelseaLoxley

IF YOU ENJOYED THIS BOOK:

Please take a moment to leave a review,
    Thank you!

Made in the USA
Coppell, TX
08 July 2022

79703905R00100